PASTIMES AND PLEASURES IN THE TIME OF JANE AUSTEN

SARAH JANE DOWNING

AMBERLEY

Cover illustration and left: London Spring Fashions, Full Dress, from La Belle Assemblée, May 1806. A splendid web Fourreau, Grecian front gown, sleeves and train bound with embossed ribband, and trimmed with tulle; a white satin slip is worn underneath. Head-dress of Circassian turban embroidered in silver lamé with a bird of paradise plume in front.

Opposite: *Le Collin Maillard*, or blind-man's buff, Plate 15 from *Le Bon Genre* (*c.* 1802), a series of observations of fashionable Parisian life at the beginning of the nineteenth century.

First published 2021

Amberley Publishing
The Hill, Stroud,
Gloucestershire, GL5 4EP

www.amberley-books.com

ISBN: 978 1 4456 7779 8 (print)
ISBN: 978 1 4456 7780 4 (ebook)

British Library Cataloguing in Publication Data.
A catalogue record for this book is available from the British Library.

Typeset in 10pt on 13pt Celeste.
Origination by Amberley Publishing.
Printed in the UK.

Contents

Introduction

Just as the fashions of Jane Austen's era and the broader Regency period define it as a unique moment in history, so do the pleasures and pastimes. The revolutions of the eighteenth century had led to radical developments in science, culture and politics, which saw society upended. The Industrial Revolution and all the new wealth it engendered created a new wealthy middle class with a vast disposable income and time to fill. New wealth had an insatiable desire for new pleasures and pastimes to enjoy and display it, and for those who were not obligated to participate in the daily grind of labour, there were pastimes and hobbies to fill every moment.

'Public Promenade Dress' invented by Mrs Bell and engraved for *La Belle Assemblée* (No. 123, 1 June 1819). Designed for the fashionable promenading hour of 5 p.m., this gorgeous walking ensemble features the slightly shorter skirt length that became popular towards the end of the decade, along with a glorious bonnet with huge bloom.

Each occasion brought the exciting opportunity for the pleasure of choosing a new outfit or ensemble, and many wardrobes expanded exponentially with an abundance of new clothes and accessories. Daytime attire was augmented with outfits specially designed for everything from carriage rides, walking in the park and visiting spas and seaside towns to attending art galleries. Evening dress, as well as gowns for balls and the opera, also meant choosing gowns for visiting, for dinner, and for the assembly rooms, with different variations required according to location.

With the rise of English fashion came the rise of the fashion magazine. *La Belle Assemblée* and *Ackermann's Repository of Arts, Literature and Fashion* quickly became essential reading and key arbiters of style. Their beautiful fashion plates depict outfits for every conceivable occasion, including those for visiting the most fashionable destinations like Vauxhall Gardens, and to celebrate momentous events such as the Battle of Waterloo with the stylish 'Waterloo Walking Dress'.

Just as leisure activities were essential for structuring society and furthering relationships, so are they pivotal in the plot, characterisation and action in Jane's novels. She frequently uses leisure activities to frame scenes or define characters. She uses the ball or the assembly rooms to allow characters to meet and form impressions of each other, and she uses activities like performing theatricals or playing games to reveal subtext or a character's hidden agenda.

'Waterloo Walking Dress', *La Belle Assemblée* (No. 73, 1 August 1815). Published only a few weeks after the Battle of Waterloo, 'the body and sleeves, composed of an intermixture of black satin and clear muslin, are exquisitely fancied; they are made in a style of novelty, elegance, and simplicity which we never recollect being equalled in the mourning costume'. It could also be worn without the undershirt for dinner parties.

The hallmark of the wider Regency era is revolution, from the American Revolution of 1775, the year of Jane Austen's birth, to the Industrial Revolution, which escalated throughout the era. The French Revolution sent a ripple of fear through English society and precipitated an age of war that lasted throughout Jane's life. No family was left untouched; generations of sons were sent to fight, with many never to return. This necessarily changed family structures of inheritance and of dependence. With such a reduced number of eligible men, competing for matrimonial prospects assumed vital importance, especially as in so many cases one good marriage could make all the difference for a whole family of siblings.

Perhaps it was also this devastating blow to the old order that escalated the development of polite society where those of lesser birth, but greater wealth, could be accepted by members of the exclusive echelons, marry into aristocratic families and even serve as Members of Parliament.

The leisured classes increased considerably in number during Jane's era. Aside from king and court, aristocracy and nobility, the genteel ranks of polite society were swelling each year with increasing numbers of professionals and newly wealthy industrialists. None of them were subject to the daily grind of work. Gentlemen ran their estates to make a profit, and professionals in law and medicine often had an independent income, as did many in

Godmersham Park in the County of Kent by W. Watts, 1785. This is how Jane would have known her brother Edward's home during her frequent visits between 1798 and 1813. She wrote to Cassandra that she loved the place for its 'elegance & ease & luxury' and perhaps the inspiration it brought. Certainly her many months spent there provided prestigious social opportunities and insight into life in a great country house and management of a large estate.

the military. Naval officers like Jane's brothers Frank and Charles would benefit from prize money for their successes, and clergymen like her father would traditionally have some small claim on their family estates in addition to the tithes they received from the Church.

The concept of polite society extended to include the new breed of well-educated industrialists and some of those whose family had made their money, but only if they had distanced themselves by several generations and had acquired a polished veneer of elegance. Below them schoolteachers and apothecaries, those in trade, shopkeepers and publicans, tenant farmers, servants and inevitably the poor were all excluded without any hope of entry.

Although the leisured classes had much of their time free to do as they pleased, their choices were deemed an indicator of good character or lack thereof. All of Jane's finest characters fill their time with public office, serving the community and the poor, or educational activities, or crafts to please their families. It is only her more louche characters such as Tom Bertram in *Mansfield Park* who indulges in anything as rakish as gambling, and although Jane and most of her genteel class disapprove, those within the Prince Regent's circle continued to cling to a more eighteenth-century roister-toistering lifestyle of heavy drinking and gambling. Some aristocratic sons saw themselves almost honour bound to indulge themselves in profligate misbehaviour as a metaphorical slap

'Messrs. Lackington, Allen & Co. Temple of the Muses, Finsbury Square', published in *Ackermann's Repository of Arts*, April 1809. Under the sign 'the cheapest bookshop in the world' Lackington proudly presented 500,000 volumes to a voracious reading public under a vast dome providing natural light to several floors and lounging rooms where readers, including the young poet John Keats, would sample before purchasing.

in the face to anyone who thought that the dour democrats who wanted to limit their privilege had a point.

Generally, though, as the nineteenth century opens, especially after Waterloo, gentlemen are prized more for their learning than their daring. A beautiful lady with a scandalous secret is still one of the most fascinating topics of conversation, yet she is unlikely to be invited to any respectable occasion. There are exceptions, of course, and the handsome war hero and poet Lord Byron is perhaps the greatest.

Kensington Garden Walking Dress, for La Belle Assemblée July 1809. People were encouraged to dress well for the gardens so close to Kensington Palace but this ensemble was exceptionally eye-catching! Consisting of: 'A spenser bodice of pale pink sarsnet. White muslin dress, with double row of scollop lace forming a light flounce round the bottom, over which is worn a black lace mantle and train.

1

Pleasure in the Picturesque

As the eighteenth century drew to its dramatic close England became enamoured with the picturesque. Previously those privileged with taking the Grand Tour throughout Europe had completed their education by enjoying the classical architecture of Greece, the remarkable curiosity of Pompeii, the romance of Venice, and the exotic pleasures of Constantinople.

'A Sea Coast Promenade Fashion' designed and executed for *La Belle Assemblée* (No. 50, 1 October 1809). Recorded as 'a Dress worn by a Lady of Rank on The Steine at Brighton,' with 'a bonnet composed of yellow satin and lace, richly embossed with leopard spots in deep orange; the front in the tiara form, a robe of yellow craped muslin, made to sit tight to the figure, A zephyr cloak of rich lace, falling in long points to the feet. Yellow Morocco sandals; gloves of York tan'.

As war with Napoleon raged across Europe, tourism – even for education – was inevitably curtailed.

William Gilpin's writings on the picturesque cleverly captured the learned and inquisitive spirit of the Grand Tour, but applied it to the natural environment close at hand. Henry Austen wrote in his 'Biographical Notice' of his sister that she was 'enamoured of Gilpin on the picturesque'. She ranks him as 'one of those first of men' in her *The History of England* and mentions his *Tour to the Highlands* in *Love and Friendship*.

Earlier writers, such as Edmund Burke in his *A Philosophical Enquiry into the Origin of our Ideas of the Sublime and the Beautiful*, had made the natural environment seem almost daunting and distant whereas Gilpin promoted an accessible relationship with where, like Lizzie Bennet in *Pride and Prejudice*, it was possible to enjoy the picturesque by simply walking through it.

Previous centuries had taught that the natural environment was something to be controlled. Spaces were designed and manicured into formal gardens more often enjoyed from a window seat than on foot, or they were dominated and cut into submission by agriculture and mining. The Industrial Revolution was cutting a swathe across Britain's green and pleasant land, and the brutality of change forced a reassessment of the values

'London Fashionable Dress', *The Lady's Magazine* (c. 1800). A desire to emulate and celebrate the neoclassical taste informs every detail from the Romanesque chaise longue to the crescent moon 'Diana' diadem.

'Promenade Dress', *Ackermann's Repository of Arts* (September 1809). Described as a 'Promenade Sea-Beach costume', it is wonderfully international. 'A Grecian frock of fine French cambric ... Roman back ... Flemish bonnet ... Chinese parasol, and a marine scarf, of purple Spanish silk, with rich ends, and border of happily contrasted shades, thrown over the figure in true Grecian elegance'. Her lemon-yellow kid shoes, however, appear to be firmly planted on the Jurassic Coast, her left foot seemingly upon a fossil.

and aesthetics of the natural world that would be reflected in everything from garden design to Turner's emotionally charged depictions of the modern world.

An age of grief and famine, with the explosion of Mount Tamarua Gothic themes, had permeated literature, art, architecture and garden design since the mid-eighteenth century, inspired in part by the fascinating sights of Continental Europe as viewed on the Grand Tour. The mood of mourning allowed sensibilities to focus on what was lost, and the glassless windows of broken abbeys and the jutting rocks of post-volcanic landscapes claimed new meaning and metaphor as they hinted at chaos and the story of cultures or families once great, now smashed. It became fashionable to take long walks engaging with the view, and if you couldn't get to Europe there were many ruins to be seen in this green and pleasant land – almost a growing number as industrialisation ravaged the landscape. During the poverty of the war and post-war years landowners built follies and artistic ruins to create work for those who had none, and many of the pleasure gardens prided themselves on realistic recreations of ruins like Palmyra, or fantasy ruined abbeys or castles.

Where independent spirits like Lizzie Bennet were happy just to enjoy the picturesque with little consideration to muddy hems or messed hair, fashion magazines published an array of beautiful walking dresses featuring mini-Elizabethan ruffs or slashed sleeves, romantic touches just perfect for the romance of history and particularly popular between 1814 and 1820.

The picturesque also encompassed political philosophy as land enclosures forced subsistence farmers to leave the land that their families had farmed for centuries, and

'A Design for a Flower Garden' from Humphrey Repton's influential 1803 book *Observations on the Theory and Practice of Landscape Gardening.*

The West Window of Tintern Abbey by Henry Gastineau, *c*. 1830. William Wordsworth immortalised Tintern Abbey in his 1798 poem 'Lines Composed a Few Miles Above Tintern Abbey', but it was already a major attraction, drawing hundreds of tourists and picnickers to sail along the River Wye to enjoy its Gothic romance.

'A Walking Dress for Autumn' from *Ackermann's Repository of Arts* (1 October 1815). The perfect ensemble for enjoying the picturesque, described as 'an open pelisse, composed of French grey sarsnet, lined with the salmon colour; the upper part of the sleeve [s]lashed with satin of corresponding colour' with 'a full ruff of needle-work', and of course a book of poetry – almost undoubtedly Jane's beloved Cowper.

large swathes of viable agricultural land was landscaped decoratively for a new breed of landowners more intent on success in politics than in farming. As the poet John Clare lamented:

> Inclosure came and trampled on the grave
> Of labour's rights and left the poor a slave...
>
> And birds and trees and flowers without a name
> All sighed when lawless law's enclosure came.

He was one of a generation who saw their land, and with it their lives, rationalised out of existence. The lot of the rural poor had by no means been easy, but the generous camaraderie with which they had shared their subsistence was what sustained them, and the laughter of children playing in the woods as their parents worked in the fields was far more nourishing than any wages could ever be. Tragically, Clare succumbed to the anomie that blights people when they are torn from their culture, tradition and existence. In 1837 he was diagnosed with 'madness' and sent to an asylum.

Jane was also painfully aware of the issues surrounding enclosure, and as a country girl she saw the consequences first-hand, especially during her visit to her Cooke cousins at Great Bookham in 1814 when she was writing *Emma*. Almost 3 million acres of British common land and heath was enclosed between 1790 and 1820, a particular problem during the long war years when most families were without a breadwinner and desperate to survive on the scrap of land left to them. This barred children from collecting firewood let alone the odd rabbit. Landowners were encouraged to grow stout, spiky hedges around their land and to make sure that none of the plants used were fruit-bearing as it wouldn't do to encourage the poor to rely on free food.

The theory of the picturesque encouraged thought about the environment, but more than that it encouraged feeling. The emotional response of artists such as Claude and poets such as Wordsworth were venerated, and thousands of amateur artists travelled to the most popular sites to ply their brush.

One fantastic accessory frequently taken was the Claude glass, a slightly convex mirror of black that captured an image of nature cast in mysterious shadow. This was used to frame a perfect picturesque, romantic, or Gothic scene – whichever the artist sought to capture. There were a variety of glasses in shades of blue and grey and they became popular enough during the 1790s to be satirised by playwrights of the day.

Everyone aspired to be if not an artist then a decent watercolourist, able to adequately capture the magical beauty and awe-inspiring history of a scene. In 1796 one of the first publications by Rudolph Ackermann – who went on to found the *Repository of Arts* magazine – was a drawing book, *Lessons for Beginners in the Fine Art*. He had founded a drawing school at No. 101 The Strand, just a few doors away from Somerset House, the home of the Royal Academy and its schools where he was master to eighty students, but his drawing books giving instruction and coloured aquatint examples of how to compose landscapes sold in their thousands. Where watercolour landscapes were one of the best ways to record the mood of a picturesque scene or a rosy-tinged sunset, the amateur artist did more serious work at home.

'Morning Dress', *Ackermann's Repository of Arts* (November 1824). Possibly the *Repository*'s ideal reader, she is stylishly dressed in an ensemble of what is probably Ackermann's own colour creation of 'Manchester Brown' while sketching no doubt using Ackermann's signature range of artists' materials.

Lith Partenope, *When Only I Have the Lineaments I Am Sure of the Effect*. A curious caricature dating to the late 1820s depicting an artist with extensive technical equipment, including camera obscura and camera lucida, attempting to capture the majesty of Vesuvius in the Bay of Naples. A pastiche of the notion that scientific optical equipment could help an artist capture the romance of nature.

It was one thing to wander through picturesque landscapes lonely as a cloud, it was quite another to experience travel at speed. Keeping a stable of fine horses and displaying expertise in riding and driving them was incredibly valuable as a mark of status for any young gentleman. To be judged a 'neck or nothing rider' or a 'capital whip' would give great kudos, as would owning a fashionable carriage drawn by an expensive matched pair, four or even six beautiful high-stepping horses.

Originally called the Whip Club, the Four Horse Club was established in 1808 by a group of aristocratic enthusiasts. Only men proven to be skilled at driving a team of four were eligible to join and attend the meets where they drove the 20 miles from Park Lane to Harrow on the Hill for a sumptuous lunch. They wore an extravagant uniform that was widely emulated by the droves of men who wanted to look like dashing 'bucks'. Rather too loud to suit the taste of Beau Brummell, they wore a kerseymere waistcoat that was vividly striped with inch-wide strips of yellow and blue, topped by a blue cut-away redingote jacket with bright brass buttons, along with tight white corduroy breeches, top boots, a white muslin cravat spotted with black, topped by a white driving coat with a remarkable fifteen capes and two tiers of pockets.

Lady Lyttelton, Sarah Spencer, writes of the Barouche Club gentry in a letter in 1810: 'A set of hopeless young men who think of no earthly thing but how to make themselves like coachmen ... have formed themselves into a club, inventing new slang words, adding new capes to their great-coats and learning to suck a quid of tobacco and chew a wisp of straw...'

Jane was also less than enamoured. While Tom Bertram in *Mansfield Park* is something of a buck, his costume remains with the gentlemanly norm. Instead, it is strident and odious John Thorpe in *Northanger Abbey* who she characterises as 'a stout young man, of middling height, who, with a plain face and ungraceful form seemed fearful of being too handsome, unless he wore the dress of a groom, and too much like a gentleman unless he were easy where he ought to be civil, and impudent where he might be allowed to be easy'.

Regency buck fashion plate from *Journal des Dames et des Modes, Costume Parisien* (1808), Plate 940, possibly by Vernet and described as *'Redingote de Drap avec Collette et Revers en Velours'*, but what Jane might consider to be 'the dress of a groom.

In *Northanger Abbey* John Thorpe is a terrible bore about his carriage, forcing Catherine to endure hours of tedious stories of his racing exploits and driving prowess. This kind of conversation would undoubtedly have been very familiar, as to be a capital whip or nonesuch were great preoccupations of the age. The final years of the eighteenth century saw an abundance of new carriage designs, from the sedate barouche, just perfect for elegant driving in St James' Park, to the elegant phaeton, so fashionable that it was featured in a fashion plate in Heideloff's *Gallery of Fashion* in 1794.

It was named after Phaethon in Greek mythology, son of the sun god Helios, who drew the chariot of the sun across the sky, almost setting the world on fire. The small carriage with seating for two, set up high, was perfect for driving in town, cutting a dash along the most elegant avenues and crescents. A gentleman or lady could drive a phaeton herself, and many were accomplished drivers, although it was considered unacceptable to go anywhere unaccompanied or without the correct servants in attendance. Feminine displays of speed or precision – 'driving to the inch' – were also forbidden in town or in public, but in the privacy of their own country estates there were more than a few female whips.

Lady Sarah Archer was famous for her elaborate make-up regime in the 1780s, at a time when many beauties were seeking a more natural look. The sight of her fiery rouge juxtaposed with her unfortunately hooked nose was a delight for caricaturists like Rowlandson and she was regularly parodied. As a friend of the Prince Regent she thought nothing of speeding through town, as he and many of his circle were known to do, but this was also fuel for the satirists and she was regularly caricatured as 'Phaetona', speeding in

Ladies in a phaeton from Heideloff's *Gallery of Fashion* (*c.* 1794). Heideloff's illustrations were not only beautiful they were aspirational and fun. In this the young women depicted enjoy one of the most stylish and luxurious carriages of the day, as well as a thrilling frisson of independence.

her sporty high-perch phaeton to the Perfumery, which was well stocked with everything from rouge to mouse skin eyebrows.

The curricle was perhaps the fastest of all, and definitely the most flash. Named for the curriculum, the racing chariot of Ancient Rome, the tiny semicircular curricle perched on two wheels could be drawn by four horses for maximum speed. It was the favourite of Robert 'Romeo' Coates, the only dandy of West Indian Caribbean extraction. His origins in Antigua were shrouded in mystery but, with his penchant for furs and diamonds, he was clearly wealthy. He was welcomed in the highest echelons of London society and he cut a dash in his maroon curricle, which was drawn by two white horses and emblazoned with his coat of arms of a cock crowing to which all the ragamuffin children shouted 'cock-a-doodle-doo' each time he drove past.

If speed was a thrill, aeronautical flight was a death-defying stunt that became an essential experience. Lunardi, the handsome young aeronaut and Italian diplomat, had a sense of showmanship and fun. He made his first ascent in London in 1784 with a cat, dog and a picnic; the crowd were sceptical, with some believing it to be a hoax and some assuming that an ascent to the heavens was inevitably one way. He had a super time drinking the wine until he felt himself 'filled with calm delight', but unfortunately sand from the ballast got in the picnic and he had to come down over Ware because the cat caught cold. He called out to a group of harvesters to catch his rope, but they ran away from his 'Devil's horse' and a woman working in the brewhouse came to his rescue. He was such a hit with the ladies

'Driving Without a Beau', a caricature of Lady Sarah Archer dashing to the Perfume Warehouse where the window display includes 'Ivory Teeth' and 'Mouse skin Eye Brows'. Her fierce independence and financial autonomy made her a target for critics and caricaturists.

Lunardi's Balloon by Robert Dighton. Lunardi equipped his balloon for the air voyage with wings to create a breeze if becalmed, and oars to lower it somehow – seemingly by rowing it in a downwards direction.

that he was commemorated in fashion with the Lunardi hat – a high crown puffed on a framework of wire – for the more modest ladies, and Lunardi garters for those less modest.

While ballooning remained a spectator activity, the hobby horse was embraced as a modern scientific form of travel. The hobby horse, dandy horse, or velocipede, was conceived in 1817 by German inventor Karl Freiherr von Drais as an answer to the rising cost of horse feed in the wake of the poor harvest following 1816 – 'the year without a summer' – when Europe remained under shadow after the volcanic eruptions in Indonesia. His dream of superseding the need for horses was never fulfilled, but the machine was exhibited throughout Europe to curious audiences, and once Covent Garden coach maker Denis Johnson procured one he quickly made his own version and applied for the British patent in 1818.

Johnson's Pedestrian Curricle had larger wheels to allow for greater speed and a steering mechanism that allowed the rider to steer with the handlebars while leaning to rest the forearms on a padded breast board. Forward momentum was created as the rider pushed away with the feet, swinging the legs in a wide running movement to propel the rider forward. It was quite easy to coast along on smooth flat terrain – swooping down hill was a breeze; however, inclines must have caused most riders to dismount and catch their breath.

Johnson even set up riding schools in the Strand and Soho so that prospective customers could take their first faltering steps in private. He also developed a dropped-frame version so ladies could also ride without having to dishevel their skirts. There was also the Pilentum, made by Hancock & Co. of Pall Mall (and named after the Latin for the covered

'Johnson, the First Rider on the Pedestrian Hobbyhorse', published by R. Ackermann (May 1819). Although Johnson appears troubled by riding his invention, those in the background are thrilled to be zipping along at high speed.

carriage used to transport religious statues or Roman ladies attending religious devotions). Also known as the 'Ladies' Accelerator', it was for more dainty use. Like a tricycle, the fair damsel was seated between the wheels, controlling the momentum with treadle boards, while in front of her a third wheel, controlled by wires extended to her reach, was used for steering.

The idea of being able to propel oneself at 10 miles an hour was compelling and particularly suited to the dandy taste. It was a great way to display a long, lean leg in the narrow trousers that were with instep strap fashionable at the time.

Although the clatter of hobby horses was heard throughout 1818 and 1819, the craze faded quickly. The health warnings against it – suggesting it was responsible for causing ruptures and hernias – may have been a factor, but it was probably the merciless attention of the satirists that drove the hobby out of fashion. Without any braking mechanism except dragging the feet on the ground, there were more than a few accidents, which led to the enactment of bylaws against the hobby horse in London. Perhaps it was this ban that effectively ended the fashion.

The Ladies' Accelerator or 'Les Draisiennes a Londres en 1819', Views of the Lady's Pedestrian Hobbyhorse published by R. Ackermann May, 1819. As if to compensate for the lesser speed, the Ladies' Accelerator was more comfortable with an upholstered arm rest.

2

Pleasure Destinations

Once the natural environment had been appreciated at the seaside and spa resort, there were a host of other more modern pastimes that first appeared during the Regency era. In addition to parks and pleasure gardens, zoos like those at Regent's Park and the Tower of London became popular. There was an equestrian show at Astley's Amphitheatre that

The Grand Orchestra at Vauxhall Gardens by A. C. Pugin and J. Bluck from Ackermann's *Microcosm of London* (1809). Dancing under the glittering lights and the clear night sky at Vauxhall was one of London's – if not life's – greatest pleasures.

Jane visited with her brothers while in London, and subsequently wrote in *Emma* of the Knightlys attending. Those with a greater taste for curiosities could see the most exotic animals – their taxidermied versions, at least – at Bullock's Museum in Piccadilly. A heightened interest in architecture and garden design led to the fashionable occupation of visiting grand houses, as Lizzie does when visiting Pemberley in *Pride and Prejudice*. There was also shopping, which during this period of import and innovation graduated from necessity to a pleasurable pastime, especially in fashionable places like London or Bath.

It was Dr Russell whose experiments with Pliny's theory of the medicinal qualities of seashells that led him to discover the medicinal value of seawater. His cure was so popular that in 1754 he was able to build himself a beautiful house on the south side of the Steine to be close to his patients throughout the bathing season.

In addition to drinking the water he recommended full immersion, and it was perhaps the bracing physical nature of the treatment, as well as the as yet unspoilt prettiness of the town, that encouraged Brighton's rakish air. Even by the 1760s there were more young men with spyglasses trained on the dozen or so bathing machines than there were using them for their correct nautical purpose.

The king's brother, the Duke of Cumberland, came to Brighton to rent Dr Russell's former home in 1779. On difficult terms with George III, he almost made a point of annoying him with his rakish existence, spending vast sums on his extensive stable of racehorses and

'Seaside Bathing Dress', invented by Mrs Bell for *La Belle Assemblée* No. 73 (1 August 1815). Ready to take advantage of the bathing machines below, Mrs Bell's clever invention 'is so contrived that the stays, petticoat, and pelisse are all put on in a few moments. A flounce of green gauze, crape, or muslin, edged with an exceedingly pretty silk trimming, ornaments the dress; which, when on, is so finished and elegant that no one could suppose it was possible to adjust it in a few moments'.

Right: 'Watering Place Morning Dress', Heideloff's *Gallery of Fashion* (1795). White was typical for morning wear, in this case teamed with wonderful pea green gloves and shoes – perhaps for Lyme Regis or maybe even Sanditon.

Below: A card for 'Sayer's Bathing Machine' at Margate, 1791. The bather would go to John and Mercy Sayer's Bathing Room on the seafront to wait for the bathing machine to be drawn up to the steep wooden steps that led down into the sea. The giant hood or umbrella of the machine would allow them to enter and enjoy the water unseen.

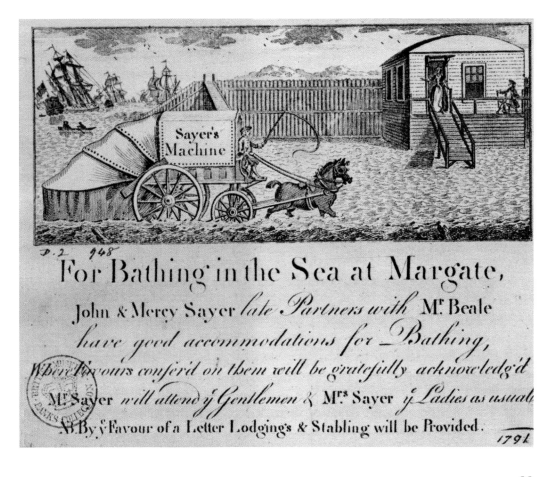

For Bathing in the Sea at Margate,

John & Mercy Sayer *late Partners with* Mr. Beale
have good accommodations for Bathing,
Where Favours confer'd on them will be gratefully acknowledg'd
Mr. Sayer *will attend y Gentlemen* & Mrs. Sayer *y Ladies as usual*
N.B By y Favour of a Letter Lodgings & Stabling will be Provided.

1791

even more on drinking and gambling. In the Hanover tradition, the Prince Regent was even more at odds with his strict father, and the moment he reached his majority he fled from court to spend time at Brighton with his uncle.

The prince enjoyed himself so much in Brighton that he must have been overjoyed when the following summer his physician diagnosed him with a 'scrophulous humour', which conveniently required a course of sea bathing. In July 1784 he set out from Carlton House in his new 'Randem' phaeton, drawn by three horses, and made the 108-mile trip to Brighton and back in ten hours, thus endorsing the passion for speed that was to become one of the greatest pleasures of the Regency rake.

His royal endorsement of the races at Lewes and Brighton Downs gave a new reason for the exodus from London for the summer season. In the years before the French Revolution, it became *de rigeuer* among deposed French aristocrats to congregate there to indulge their passion for English horses and carriages as the height of style à l'*Anglaise.*

Where once Bath was almost as fashionable as London, each season brimming with the fabulous and the fascinating (Fanny Burney spent her time there with Mrs Thrale and Queen Charlotte), by Jane's day it was a respectable home for desperate gentility where you could still appear relatively grand even while eking out a small budget. It was a city of invalids, hypochondriacs and spinsters, as Sir Walter Elliot laments in *Persuasion*:

> The worst of bath was, the number of its plain women. He did not mean to say that there were no pretty women, but the number of plain was out of all proportion. He had frequently observed, as he walked, that one handsome face would be followed by thirty, or five and thirty frights; and once, as he had stood in a shop in bond-street, he had counted eighty seven women go by, one after another, without there being a tolerable face among them ... there certainly were a dreadful multitude of ugly women in bath; and as for the men – they were infinitely worse!

Racing by H. Alken (1820). Due to royal patronage, even the genteel would join the vast crowds attending races, but ladies would be more inclined to retain the safe vantage point of their carriages.

Right: 'Morning Walking or Carriage Costume', *Ackermann's Repository of Arts* (1 December 1810). There do not appear to have been any designs dedicated to going to the races, but this ensemble of black round robe worn with white habit shirt and a black or grey cardinal mantle and Prussian helmet, both lined in ermine, would have been suitably warm, as well as understatedly elegant.

Below: A haven for those less active, libraries were vitally important at every seaside and spa resort. *The Lending Library at Scarborough* by Thomas Rowlandson, after Green, appeared in *Poetical Sketches of Scarborough in 1813* alongside these lines:

> As in life's tide by careful fate
> The mind is made to circulate
> Just so each watering place supplies
> It's CIRCULATING LIBRARIES:
> Where charming volumes may be had
> Of good indifferent and bad
> And some small towns on Britain's shore
> Can boast of book shops half a score
> Scarbro and with much truth may boast
> Her's good as any on our coast
> AINSWORTH'S or SCAUM'S no matter which
> Or WHITING'S all in learning rich
> Afford a more than common measure
> Of pleasant intellectual treasure

Although entitled 'Bathing Place Evening Dress', the description within the text of *La Belle Assemblée* (1 September 1810) is 'A Fashionable Sea-Side Walking Dress', 'A gown of white French cambric, or pale pink muslin, hemmed round the bottom with three rows of deep Mechlin lace; made rather short, and worn over trousers of white French cambric, which are trimmed the same as the bottom of the dress.' This plate is unusual for the error in the title, but even more so as this is perhaps the first fashion plate to depict a woman in trousers.

Jane had enjoyed visiting Bath during the 1790s but was less keen about living there. When choosing where to live in Bath in 1801 Jane expressed a preference for No. 4 Sydney Place: 'It would be very pleasant to be near Sydney gardens, we might go into the labyrinth every day!'

Planned by Baldwin as the main feature to the Pulteney estate and spanning 12 acres, the hexagonal Sydney Gardens was the largest pleasure garden outside of London. Entered via the Sydney Hotel, the elegant tree-lined walks are decorated with variegated lamps among the thatched pavilions. The sylvan delights within included grottoes, waterfalls and two Chinese-style iron bridges built over the canal.

In his *Walks Through Bath* (1819) Pierce Egan says: 'The Labyrinth, shown here at three-pence each person, is an object of curiosity. The inducement to enter it is one of Merlin's swings, which appears not only very prominent, but easy of access. However, it might puzzle any cunning person, if left to himself and without a clue, for six hours, to acquire the much wished for spot; and it is rather a difficult task when the explorer of the Labyrinth has the direction pointed out to him from a man stationed in the swing. The inns and outs necessary to be made, it is said, measure half a mile.'

This might be why Jane enjoyed Sydney on 21 April 1805: 'Yesterday was a busy day with me, or at least with my feet & my stockings; I was walking almost all day long; I went to Sydney gardens soon after one, & did not return til four.'

Right: 'Cheltenham Summer Dress' engraved for *La Belle Assemblée* (No. 49, September 1809). Described as a 'Walking Dress': a 'Round dress of jaconet muslin, made tight to the shape, slashed Spanish front, laced with ribband; bosom and sleeves composed of hail-stone spotted msulin; train sloped up in front à-la-Parisienne,' but worn with practical 'gaitered slippers of blue kid'.

Below: Sydney Gardens, Bath by J. C. Nattes (1805). The most beautiful, stylish and prestigious of all the provincial pleasure gardens, it was Jane Austen's favourite and where she walked every day while staying at Sydney Place.

Sydney expertly rode the cusp between old and new, with all the fantasy of romantic ruins and a hermit's cot and elegant public breakfasting each day, but also with the new taste for firework concerts, balloon ascents, walking, riding and daytime activities, which were later to become the hallmark of the Victorian gardens.

Although the pleasure gardens had long provided a pretty place for an elegant promenade with good, well-sanded walks to allow for wearing pretty shoes, with the low heels that became popular in the 1790s, there was less need as walking became a more serious business.

Boots were also modish. Emma is told in *The Watsons*: 'nothing sets off a neat ankle more than a half boot; Nankin galoshed with black looks very well.' These would be mid-calf-length, lace-up boots in a tough yellowy-brown cotton fabric, with the galosh being a section of black leather around the base of the foot, joined to the sole to keep the damp and mud out. She replied that 'unless they are so stout as to injure their beauty, they are not fit for Country walking'.

'Promenade Dress', *Ackermann's Repository of Arts* (July 1811). Perfect for the English summer: 'A white jaconet muslin high dress of walking length,' a shorter length to keep mud and damp at bay, 'ornamented round the bottom, cuffs, and collar with a Tuscan border in tambour,' which would give the delicate fabric extra substance. 'A sea green sarsnet spencer' would provide a modicum of warmth and 'half boots similar in shade' more substantial for walking, especially over wet grass, with both a Chinese parasol and 'a large transparent white veil thrown over the whole' to protect from the sun.

Throughout the eighteenth century, Vauxhall Pleasure Gardens reigned supreme as one of the most remarkable venues ever open to the public. Situated by the River Thames, visitors would escape life's mundanities as they sailed across the moonlit river. They would make an elegant entrance walking along a tree-lined path, the shady boughs laden with strings of coloured lights, to arrive in the grove where a spectacular illuminated bandstand presided. The edges were spanned by rows of private supper boxes, each with a painting by Francis Hayman and the novelty of serving dinner oneself without the aid of servants.

Each walk radiating from the grove gently meandered to a classical statue, obelisk, or picturesque ruin. Providing purpose and inspiring conversation, these focal points allowed gentlemen to demonstrate their knowledge and share anecdotes of the Grand Tour, and for ladies to exhibit their elegant, good taste.

Fashion was hugely important when visiting the pleasure gardens as the walks and colonnades, beautifully laid out for promenading, were also remarkably effective as a catwalk. Walking was the most fashionable form of exercise, and what could be better than walking in a beautiful pleasure garden where the wide pathways were clean, even and neatly sanded.

'Vauxhall Vittoria Fête Dress', *La Belle Assemblée* (1 October 1813). One of the most spectacular and notorious occasions at the pleasure gardens was the Vittoria fête at Vauxhall Gardens. One of the highlights of the season, it completely sold out, with black-market tickets being sold at £15 each – the equivalent of £700 today. The fête was later depicted by Thomas Hardy in his epic poem about the Napoleonic Wars, 'The Dynasts'. A total of 14,000 people attended and it was said that the melee in trying to get coaches at the end of the night was as bad as the battle itself.

By the end of the eighteenth century there were sixty-four pleasure gardens in London, with others appearing in the burgeoning industrial cities like Birmingham, Manchester and Liverpool. Many claimed the title 'Vauxhall' in the hopes of capturing something of the kudos of the now legendary London Vauxhall to bring sparkle to their concerts, balls, public breakfasts and firework displays.

The romantic sensibilities of the pleasure gardens began to dwindle as recession hit after the Napoleonic Wars, and the fountains, statuary and romantic ruined castles of the eighteenth century began to be replaced by entertainment that offered thrills and spectacle. Hot-air balloon ascents became all the rage, but if the sight of man defying gravity wasn't enough, there were full-scale battle re-enactments cast in stunning displays of fireworks.

'The Descent of Madame Saqui Surrounded by Fireworks', published by T. Kelly, No. 17 Paternoster Row, 17 May 1822. Firework events like this were ever popular at Vauxhall Gardens. On Wednesday 19 June 1799, Jane wrote to her sister Cassandra: 'Last night we were in Sydney Gardens again ... We did not go till nine, and then were in very good time for the fireworks, which were really beautiful, and surpassing my expectation.'

3

Cultural Pleasures

'Drury Lane Theatre' by A. C. Pugin and J. Bluck from Ackermann's *Microcosm of London* (1808). Opening on 13 March 1793, the new theatre was huge and with multiple staircases, exits and four above-ceiling reservoirs in case of fire – it was dedicated to safety as well as luxury. Both the king and the Prince of Wales had their own saloons there, as well as boxes for their use, which were specially decorated with crimson velvet and gold tassels when they were in attendance.

The popularity of the theatre, opera and symphony were compounded during the Regency era, with a host of new stylish venues in the popular spa towns and growing new urban metropolises. Jane visited the Lyceum in London and the Theatre Royal in Bath, and she also set scenes at the theatre in *Emma* and *Pride and Prejudice*. Yet, it is the home-made theatricals that she features more thoroughly, allowing Fanny's experience in *Mansfield Park* to become pivotal to the story. Performance of music was also vitally important to most young ladies who needed to display the talent, and many fashion plates feature aspirational instruments like the harp.

A keen interest in literature and poetry would be served by a growing number of libraries, as well as magazines, and a good command of language was essential for letter writing, an activity that took place most days for both Jane and her characters. From art at the Royal Academy to science at the Royal Institution, education was eagerly sought and enjoyed.

The Regency was an era of romping achievement, from the rise of literature and the birth of magazine culture to the glamourous new theatres and opera houses that would make even the most reluctant theatregoer feel the power of performance.

Theatre

It is clear from her sparkling comedic dialogue to her memorable characters so deftly drawn by their word and deed that Jane had an intimate knowledge of, and fondness for, the theatre. From an early age she wrote for her family theatricals, and theatre was a valuable part of her schooling. The first record of Jane attending the theatre is in a letter of August 1796: 'We are to be at Astley's tonight, which I am glad of.'

'Evening, Theatre or Opera Dress', designed by Mrs Bell for *La Belle Assemblée* (No. 64, 1 December 1814). Formal full dress was almost always white with white accessories. Mrs Bell's design is unusual for the hint of pink, probably achieved by a layer of softly striped, white tulle or gauze over a pink satin gown.

Astley's Amphitheatre of Arts, as it was known in 1796, was one of a growing number of lesser or illegitimate theatres in London who avoided the licensing laws that had since 1737 restricted legitimate theatre to two patent playhouses, the Drury Lane Theatre and the Covent Garden Theatre. Philip Astley had opened his equestrian theatre by the river in Lambeth in 1770 to exhibit equestrian feats, conjuring and fireworks. At first it was little more than an open-air circus ring with covered seats, but by 1783 when a patent was granted it had a full roof, stage and an exciting range of performances under the collective title of 'burletta'. This allowed for the occasional straight play to be added to the programme of music, songs and dancing, swordsmanship, acrobatics and, of course, equestrian events. There were thirty-five new acts in 1796 when Jane attended with the Austens, including performances from a clever little pony only 35 inches tall, as well as two Catawba Indian chiefs who gave a display of tomahawk throwing, shooting bow and arrows, and their war dance.

'Astley's Amphitheatre' by A. C. Pugin and J. Bluck from Ackermann's *Microcosm of London* (1808). At 135 feet wide, the stage was the largest in Europe, and needed to be to accommodate the troops of horses that graced it. The *Microcosm* also boasts of its remarkable scenery, machinery and vast chandeliers, but says nothing of the cleaning arrangements. The *Blood-red Knight* show was so popular and overcrowded throughout 1810 it was claimed that profits exceeded £1,000 (the equivalent of £46,500) per week.

She chose Astley's for the reconciliatory meeting between Harriet and Robert Martin in *Emma*, although it is not entirely clear whether it is the original amphitheatre or the Olympic theatre in the Strand that was also known as Astley's Pavilion from 1805 when he took on the lease. Both, however, had a convivial atmosphere where the tickets were less expensive – 4s for a box as opposed to the bitterly contested 7s at a patent theatre – and the classes mixed freely. Children particularly enjoyed the novel entertainments, which often included performing animals such as Bobby, a pony who was able to boil a kettle to serve tea.

Theatregoing was huge during the Regency. When both the Drury Lane and Covent Garden theatres were rebuilt in 1808 and 1809 after disastrous fires, they seated over 3,000. So cavernous were these spaces that Sarah Siddons referred to 'old monster', and a particular formal, artificial style of performance developed, as much for the necessity of projecting to the back rows far in the distance as conforming to a stilted notion of Shakespeare.

OPERA DRESS.

Nº 29. of R.ACKERMANN'S REPOSITORY of ARTS &c. Pub. May 1.1811. at 101 Strand. LONDON.

'Opera Dress', *Ackermann's Repository of Arts* (1 May 1811). 'A white muslin robe with an Algerine tunic of white satin trimmed with silver fringe, worn with a helmet cap of silver net and spangles with a cluster of Labrador roses adorning the front. The child's costume is designed to complement the mother's: a short frock and trowsers of plain Indian muslin with a short French tunic of white sarsnet tied at the neck with silk cord and tassels and trimmed with flounces of lace similar to the frock.'

Above: 'Opera House' by A. C. Pugin and J. Bluck from Ackermann's *Microcosm of London* (1808). Now Her Majesty's Theatre in Haymarket, at the opening of the nineteenth century it was simply known as 'The Opera House', as it was the first place that any of Mozart's operas were heard in London – *La clemenza di Tito* on 27 March 1806. Opera-going was less reverential and more social than it is today, with lively conversation and socialising during much of the performance between the arias.

Right: 'Opera Dress', *La Belle Assemblée* (1 July 1811). Her programme rests forgotten on the edge of the balcony as it is more likely that she would use her opera glass – or rather opera telescope – to inspect the company in the other boxes. It was even known for Regency audiences to breech the stage to get a better view of the fashionable and illustrious company above.

OPERA DRESS

In *Sense and Sensibility* Willoughby runs into Sir John Middleton in the lobby of the Drury Lane Theatre to discover that Marianne Dashwood is seriously ill at Cleveland. In *Pride and Prejudice*, Lydia Bennet, without a second thought about the shame of her elopement, reports that 'to be sure London was rather thin, but however the little theatre was open'. The little theatre was 'the dear enchanting Haymarket,' as Jane's niece, Fanny Knight, referred to it. They frequently went to the theatre together, preferring the Haymarket Theatre, which was of far smaller dimensions and, like many of the provincial theatres, a far better size for drama to keep its emotional intimacy.

Boydell's Shakespeare Gallery, 1789–1805

With the fantastic revivals of Shakespeare packing theatres and among the favourite subjects for private theatricals, renowned printmaker John Boydell saw the perfect opportunity to open a gallery dedicated to the bard. The Shakespeare Gallery opened at No. 52 Pall Mall on 4 May 1789 to exhibit thirty-four canvasses of Shakespearian subjects painted by the finest artists, including Sir Joshua Reynolds and Henry Fuseli, painter of *The Nightmare*, who was already renowned for historical works and Shakespearian subjects such as *Lady Macbeth Sleepwalking*.

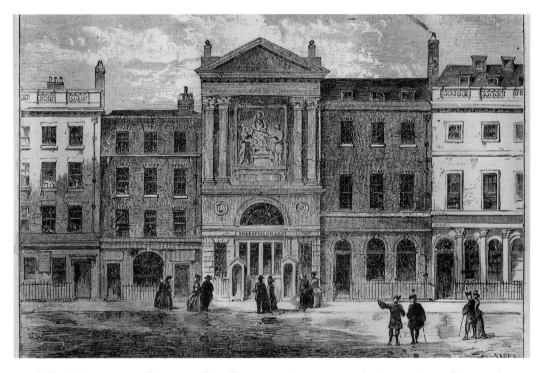

Boydell's Shakespeare Gallery in Pall Mall, *c.* 1790. George Dance's innovative architectural design echoes the passionate blending of Shakespeare and neoclassicism within. It also offers the first use of ammonite fossils as the volutes that top each pilaster would become known as the 'Ammonite Order'.

Boydell, like many others, felt that British art had become too superficial, dealing mostly with portraiture and landscape rather than more sophisticated concepts. His intention for the Shakespeare Gallery was to reinvigorate British art with the great stories of history and literature to promote a modern British school that would become internationally renowned. He promised significant rewards to the artists he commissioned – Reynolds was reputedly paid £1,000 for *Macbeth*, Act IV, Scene I, the equivalent of approximately £56,000 today – and employed some of the finest engravers to make reproductions. Following Hogarth's success in mounting an exhibition of his works to encourage subscribers to purchase his prints and folios, Boydell was confident that the gallery would promote sales of his prints. He also charged a shilling entrance fee to the exhibition just in case.

There was an informative catalogue for the exhibition, which included the passages from Shakespeare on each subject and pinpointed the exact moment that the painting depicted. As the public passed through the three large upper galleries they were thrilled by the mix of comic and tragic and the eclectic blend of renowned and unknown artists, almost inevitably selecting the prints they would choose before even reaching the shop.

Jane's friend and fellow author Fanny Burney visited the Shakespeare Gallery and mentions in her diary on 27 June 1792 that there was 'the long shop', a good-sized museum shop where prints and subscriptions were on sale to those 'patrons of native genius', as Boydell obsequiously referred to his subscribers. She might well have suggested to Jane, a fellow Shakespeare enthusiast, that she would enjoy visiting Boydell's when she was staying in nearby Cork Street in August 1796.

'Exhibition or Morning Dress' from *The Lady's Magazine* (1811). A simple ensemble complete with a quizzing glass, an elegant accessory that would allow close magnified scrutiny without having to resort to wearing the antipathy of beauty – spectacles.

Although Boydell's vision for a renaissance of history painting was hugely successful, spawning a slew of imitators, his dream of financial success did not materialise, as he said the Napoleonic Wars caused delays and prevented many of his contacts from fulfilling their promised subscription payments. Although considered a worthy endeavour to bring enlightenment to the middle classes, that gained a lot of support from illustrious patrons and the government, there was also a certain squeamishness about the vulgarity of relatively inexpensive prints available to those who couldn't afford the original paintings or illustrated folios.

The caricaturist James Gillray was also very damning in his illustration of Boydell in *Shakespeare Sacrificed or The Offering to Avarice* (June 1789), which depicted him clutching bulging bags of money while throwing copies of Shakespeare's works onto a funeral pyre. Perhaps it should be noted that Gillray had only recently been refused a commission by Boydell for the gallery.

By 1804 there were 167 paintings, and Boydell claimed to have spent an enormous £150,000 on his Shakespeare project. The Shakespeare Gallery closed in 1804 and the building was reopened as The British Institution in 1805 by a group of artists who shared his vision, but it was destroyed in 1870.

'The British Institution' by A. C. Pugin and J. Bluck from Ackermann's *Microcosm of London* (1808). Founded in 1805 to foster British talent, the Prince of Wales was vice-patron. As the *Microcosm* explains, the intention was 'to form a school of painting for the rising generation, by furnishing exemplars by the old masters, from the collections of the nobility and gentry who formed and supported the plan'. For the many pupils, both male and female, Sir Joshua Reynolds recommended that they learn by painting companion pieces to the old masters rather than just copying them.

Boydell was almost immediately copied by other London print publishers, most notably by Thomas Macklin in his Poet's Gallery, Robert Bowyer in his Historic Gallery and Henry Fuseli in his Milton Gallery, each capitalising on the trend for the emotional consumption of art that Boydell had fostered and Jane loved to observe.

The Phantasmagoria

The Phantasmagoria show opened at the Lyceum Theatre in the Strand in 1800 and remained there for two years. Monsieur de Philipsthal, who had previously exhibited the show in Paris, was at great pains to point out that his show was the only one under licence from His Majesty and visitors must accept no spurious imitations. The playbill promised to:

> Introduce the Phantoms or Apparitions of the DEAD or ABSENT, in a way more completely illusive than has ever been offered to the eye of the public Theatre, as the Objects freely originate in the Air, and unfold themselves under various Forms and Sizes such as Imagination alone has hitherto painted them, occasionally assuming the Figure and most perfect Resemblance of the Heroes and other distinguished Characters of past and present Times.
>
> This Spectrology which professes to expose the Practices of artful Impostors and pretended Exorcists ... in order to render these apparitions more interesting, they will be introduced during the progress of a tremendous thunder storm accompanied by vivid lightening hail and wind.

A mixture of *The Mysteries of Udolpho* and a live-action Fuseli painting, the show must have thrilled all Gothic sensibilities and sent the imagination reeling.

This was just the optical part of the exhibition. The *Phantasmagoria* somewhat incongruously also included mechanical pieces of art, including the *Mechanical Peacock*, 'which so exactly imitates the Actions of that stately Bird that it has frequently been thought Alive', and the *Beautiful Cossack* 'enclosed in a small Box, she opens it when ordered and presents herself to the spectators ... compliments the Company, and dances after the Manner of the Cossacks' mysteriously 'she will also resolve different Questions etc. etc.'

The *Aegyptiana* was also at the Lyceum and the playbill warns against confusing the two shows as this depiction of Egypt, a series of eighteen scenes based on Dominique Vivant Denon's illustrations for his book *Travels in Upper and Lower Egypt*, also played heavily to the macabre. The original *Fantasmagorie*, which was created by Etienne Gaspard Robertson in post-Revolutionary Paris before the Reign of Terror (the mass guillotining of the aristocrats), was completely washed from the Parisian streets, was housed in a crumbling chapel of an abandoned Capuchin monastery. Early shows drew tenacious Parisians into the darkness of the mausoleum to encounter Revolutionary figures such as Robespierre and Marat, so recently dead, whereas later shows used magic lantern effects to summon images of an Egyptian necropolis with tombs complete with mummies awoken by their unwelcome intrusion.

View of the CATACOMBS under the CITY of PARIS.

GROUND PLAN.

'View of the Catacombs under the City of Paris' (published by T. Kelly, 20 March 1822). Wearing spectral white muslin while flitting past stacks of skulls in the candlelit catacombs, this is the kind of Gothic adventure that the *Phantasmagoria* sought to replicate.

Egypt and its secrets of the dead had come to the Regency consciousness in 1798 when Nelson secured victory over Napoleon, ending his Egyptian campaign. The gilded motifs of Ancient Egypt were drawn into the language of art, architecture and interior design, but so close to the memory of the Terror the idea of the dead as-yet not departed was compelling to both grieving nations. Napoleon had made a point of amassing Egyptian treasures, seemingly hoping that the appropriation would endow him with their majesty. In 1802 the Rosetta Stone was put on display at the British Museum. It was part of a rich haul of items freshly confiscated from the emperor's forces as part of the British victory, so held particularly powerful significance.

Piccadilly also hosted its own Egyptian fantasy. William Bullock had enjoyed great success with his museum of natural and artificial curiosities in Liverpool since 1795, but when he moved his museum to London in 1809 it became the city's most popular attraction within a month and gained a record 80,000 visitors within the first year.

Bullock's Egyptian Hall

Bullock's Egyptian Hall was built in 1812 as a museum of natural history, the first to display items with some sense of their natural origin. A shilling would purchase entrance over the threshold flanked by imposing columns engraved with hieroglyphics to see the animals exhibited with correct Linnean classification and notes as to their feeding and behavioural habits. But it would cost a further shilling to venture along the corridor fashioned as a rocky cave that opened out into the Pantherion, a tropical forest comprised of models of exotic plants against panoramic backdrops.

'Bullock's Museum, Piccadilly' from *Ackermann's Repository of Arts* (June, 1810). The description extols: 'the public are indebted for one of the most refined, rational, and interesting exhibitions ... the astonished visitor is in an instant transported from the crowded streets of the metropolis to the center of a tropical forest, in which are seen as in real life, all its various inhabitants...'

Many of his specimens had been brought back by sailors, including those who had accompanied Captain Cook on his voyage to the South Seas. In 1810 British military doctor Alexander Dunlop approached Bullock, offering him the skin of a 'camel-opard'. The unfortunate creature had formerly been a giraffe and Bullock knew that once taxidermied and suitably mounted it would stand twice the height of his elephant and would become an excellent draw for his display, which according to *Bell's Weekly Messenger* in early 1810 was 'the most fashionable place of amusement in London'.

He was, however, horrified by Dunlop's other offering. Dunlop was, he said, 'in possession of a Hottentot woman' and he could offer a contract to exhibit her for the next two years. Such was 'the extraordinary shape and make of the woman' that she was guaranteed to engage the nation's curiosity and would 'make the fortune' of anyone exhibiting her. A supporter of the abolitionist movement, Bullock was appalled at the idea of exhibiting a human, especially as he was certain that it must be against her will. He declared that 'such an exhibition would not meet the countenance of the public'.

Unfortunately, he was wrong, and in October 1810 Saartjie Baartman was exhibited at No. 225 Piccadilly as 'The Hottentot Venus' by Hendrik Cesars, her 'manager'. The actor John Kemble and comedian Charles Matthews visited her and were shocked to see the way she was treated; members of the public crowded onto the stage to pinch and poke her. Kemble made a complaint about her treatment and her situation became the subject of a high-profile trial. With abolition of slavery so recently won in Britain, those of the abolitionist cause were very keen to ensure that this new breach of human rights gained no traction and Bullock was called upon to give testimony. Dunlop and Cesars also testified, claiming that Saartjie must have the right to exhibit herself in the same way as any giant or dwarf – both of whom were popular sights in Regency London. Her supporters argued that as she was exhibited in a skin-tight costume designed to give the impression of nudity to emphasise her sexual features, the intention to exploit her was clear. Although the case looked hopeful enough for her supporters to arrange her passage safely home to her family in the Cape Colony of South Africa, ultimately the court found in favour of Dunlop and Cesars, who at the eleventh hour produced a contract supposedly signed by Saartjie, even though at the time she could not even speak English let alone read or write it.

Stephano Polito didn't have any qualms about exhibiting 'exotic' people. At Bartholomew's Fair in 1790 he exhibited 'three most wonderful Wild-Born Human Beings ... found in a remote valley, adjoining the Alps'. These 'Monstrous Craws', as they were billed, were in fact people suffering with the inflated throat caused by goitre.

'Bartholomew Fair' by A. C. Pugin and J. Bluck, from Ackermann's *Microcosm of London* (1808), which described it as a 'British Saturnalia'. Some were dancing, some were fighting, and some were sampling the 'epicurean delights' of fried sausages. There were rope-dancers, fire breathers and Pidcock's Menagerie promised 'the largest elephant in the world except himself!'.

By 1792 he had graduated to animals. His travelling menagerie – a 'Grand Collection of living Birds and Beasts' – included a lion, tiger, leopard, puma and wolf, all surprisingly contained in three wagons. According to the *Stamford Mercury* on 21 March 1800, he also had 'a most surprising animal lately brought from the interior parts of Bengal, yet undescribed by naturalists' which might now be considered a sloth, later adding kangaroos, an elephant and a rhinoceros.

Many of these poor creatures were relocated to the Strand in 1810 when Polito bought Gilbert Pidcock's Menagerie at the Exeter Exchange, or the 'Change as it was affectionately known. Founded in 1788, the menagerie was well established as the only place in London to see live animals if you did not wish to go to the Tower of London, and it was one of the most popular attractions for visitors from the country.

Before popularising his 'Modern Ark' on the Strand, Gilbert Pidcock had also had a curious travelling menagerie complete with, as his advertising stated, a 'wonderful little Fairy ... he eats, drinks, likewise smoaks his pipe, and sleeps in the human way' – presumably a monkey. He also had a wagon of 'living monsters', including a two-headed cow and a three-legged colt.

'Saddlers Wells' by A. C. Pugin and J. Bluck from Ackermann's *Microcosm of London* (1808). 'The poet William Wordsworth visited and later recalled "the half-rural Sadler's Wells where he saw giants and dwarfs Clowns, conjurers, posture makers, harlequins: Amid the uproar of the rabblement, Perform their feats".'

The 'Change housed an arcade of small shops below with large galleries above divided into areas for individual species, each brightly painted with imaginary depictions of the animal in their natural habitat. Unfortunately, little consideration was given to how they might feel in cramped conditions, with prey animals forced to bunk with their predators, and there were frequent complaints from neighbours about noise, especially the roaring of lions.

The exotic animals also acted as muse for many contemporary artists and writers. George Stubbs modelled his famous *Rhinoceros* portrait of 1790 on the rhinoceros at the 'Change, and Edwin Landseer was a frequent visitor, as well as Benjamin Robert Haydon, as it was the best place to study and paint the animals from life. Lord Byron was also a regular visitor, enjoying interacting with animals such as Chunee, an Indian elephant who had enjoyed a theatrical career in London, appearing at Covent Garden Theatre and in pantomime at Sadler's Wells.

Among other talents Chunee was adroit at taking a gentleman's hat or handing him a sixpence. Byron said, 'The elephant took and gave me my money again — took off my hat — opened a door — trunked a whip — and behaved so well, that I wish he was my butler.'

Sadly, even though Chunee was hugely valuable as the star of the show, when he ran amok in 1826, killing his keeper, he was judged too dangerous to keep. There was a public outcry at the callous cruelty of his demise, firstly involving attempted poisoning but he refused to eat the poisoned food, then a firing squad of soldiers from Somerset House, and when that didn't work he was stabbed by his vet. Poor Chunee was eulogised, memorialised in poetry and a highly successful play. In April 1826, within a month of his hideously tragic death, the Zoological Society of London was formed, ensuring that shortly after the remaining animals of the 'Change were removed to better conditions at Surrey Zoological Gardens.

4

Domestic Pleasures

Georgina, Countess Bathurst (née Lennox), by Sir Thomas Lawrence *c.* 1789 when she married politician and statesman Henry Bathurst, the 3rd Earl of Bathurst. Her virtue is indicated by her intense dedication to her embroidery.

Most families would devote time to playing sports and games like shuttlecock and spillikins, as play had recently become recognised as an important part of child development. Perhaps the most time at home was spent on handicrafts such as creating silhouettes or découpage, but needlework in all its forms was by far the most popular. Much time was devoted to decorating hats, retrimming gowns, tambouring muslin or embroidering reticules, and netting was a fashionable craft even with young men. Creating beautiful needlework was a reward in itself, and Jane was very proud of her skill. The greatest value, however, was that the innovative needleworker was able to rework her wardrobe in the latest styles far more quickly than those who had to wait for the fashions to become available in the provinces.

It was important to be accomplished with a needle not only for fancy work to display taste and skill, but for more practical items for the household. Mending and making underwear and household linens would be done in the morning before guests were received. Cravats, shirts and nightshirts were made as gifts for the male members of the household. Jane and Cassandra made shirts and cravats for their brothers – for Edward in 1796 and for Charles in 1799 – and she has Fanny do the same in *Mansfield Park* so that her brother had all the linen he needs before leaving to join his naval ship:

'Fanny was very anxious to be useful and therefore set about working for Sam immediately and by working early and late, with perseverance and great dispatch, did so much, that the boy was shipped off at last, with more than half his linen ready.'

This fashion plate depicting a lady playing shuttlecock appeared in *Journal des Dames et des Modes, Costume Parisien* as Plate 1,918 in 1820, and *Corriere delle Dame* during the same year. It is extremely unusual as it is one of only a handful of fashion plates depicting any sporting activity other than riding.

Even the most aristocratic ladies would spend considerable time making clothes for the poor, especially clothes for babies and children. A gift of warm baby clothes could make all the difference for the survival of a baby in a poor rural household. Sadly, poverty was rife during the Regency due to many families losing their breadwinner to the Napoleonic Wars and many more losing their livelihoods as the march towards industrialisation destroyed many rural and craft occupations.

In *Mansfield Park* the irascible Mrs Norris chides Fanny: 'If you have no work of your own, I can supply you from the poor basket'.

In *Persuasion* Mrs Smith made small needlework items to be sold so the proceeds could go to those in need:

> As soon as I could use my hands, she taught me to knit, which has been a great amusement, and she put me in the way of making these little thread-cases, pin-cushions and card-racks, which you always find me so busy about, and which supply with the means of doing a little good to one or two very poor families in the neighbourhood. She has a large acquaintance, of course professionally, among those who can afford to buy, and she disposes of my merchandise.

There were more than a few genteel ladies to turn to their needle to make what was termed 'pin money', but in many cases was rather more vital to survival. Many post-Revolutionary French émigrés, once having sold what remained of their own jewellery and dress accessories, took up the needle to make pretty trifles such as needle cases to sell. Fanny

'Morning Dress or Costume a la Devotion', *Ackermann's Repository of Arts* (October 1810). A very rare depiction of an ensemble for church, even though what was worn each week in full view of the community would have been extremely important. As described: 'A plain cambric high gown with surplice sleeves and Vandyke collar, a Spanish robe of pea green muslin crape or sarsnet with beehive bonnet, Limeric gloves and Spanish slippers of sea green kid.'

Dashwood buys a couple as gifts for the Misses Steele in *Sense and Sensibility*, thereby showing she had insufficient regard for them than to take the trouble to make them herself.

It was a good mark of character to display a responsible industrious nature. Making items of decoration and decor would exhibit skill, as well as levels of taste and sophisticated interests. It also did no harm to occupy the hands so they could be displayed to advantage while allowing one's mind to drift during a dull story or keeping one's gaze decorously averted to allow the intensity of eye contact to seem all the more powerful at opportune moments for flirtation. It could also be a welcome distraction in awkward moments, such as when Elizabeth received an unexpected visit from Mr Darcy and 'sat down again to her work, with an eagerness which it did not often command'.

Like all Regency ladies Jane Austen spent a portion of every day at her needlework, and she was at 'her merriest' when sewing with her companions. As with her literature, she approached it as a perfectionist, with the attitude 'an artist cannot do anything slovenly' and proud to say 'I am the neatest worker of the party'.

She wrote to her sister Cassandra in December 1808: 'I wish I could help you in your Needlework, I have two hands & a new Thimble that lead a very easy life'. To be a good needlewoman was an accomplishment required of every young lady regardless of class, with training beginning in childhood working samplers. Jane was keen to encourage her niece's sewing by making a needle case for her that was hand-painted and tied with yellow ribbons, wrapped with the note 'with aunt Jane's love'.

Fashion plate depicting a lady embroidering a border in bright coquelicot thread, from *Journal des Dames et des Modes, Costume Parisien* (Plate 546, An. 12, from year twelve of the Revolution – 1804). (*Cornette et Canezou a Garnitures Plissées*)

Such dear little items were frequently exchanged as a personal expression of affection and perhaps a sense of camaraderie between women in their creativity. Of course, it did no harm to make gifts for people with whom it would be useful to curry favour. In *Sense and Sensibility*, keen to ingratiate herself with Lady Middleton, Lucy Steele opts to make a gift for her daughter 'with an alacrity and cheerfulness which seemed to infer that she could taste no greater delight than in making a filigree basket for a spoilt child'.

Netting

Netting became hugely popular during the second half of the eighteenth century. The net, or reticulum, held a hint of the classical world as well her brother had multitude of practical uses. Using silk, fine wool or linen, a delicate elliptical shuttle and a gauge, ladies would create a variety of nets of differing density and size to create all manner of accessories. Miss Andrews in *Northanger Abbey* was 'netting herself the sweetest cloak you can conceive', a feat Catherine Morland was unlikely to match since for her 'the netting box, just leisurely drawn forth, was closed with joyful haste'. Although undoubtedly aware that by doing so she was missing an opportunity to display her industrious nature and the delicate movements of her hands, she did not have the patience or diligence of Fanny Price whose table between the windows in her room at Mansfield Park 'was covered with workboxes and nettingboxes, which had been given her at different times, principally by [her cousin] Tom'.

'Ball Dress', *Ackermann's Repository of Arts* (1 March 1810). 'A plain slip of white gossamer satin with short sleeves and square bosom. A Circassian robe of brown silk net, the meshes terminated with white or gold beads with pearl head-dress á la Diana.'

Gentlemen would also net, bringing practicality to the drawing room. Captain Harville in *Persuasion* made fishing nets and 'fashioned needlework netting-needles and pins with improvements'. Jane Austen relates that her nephews at Godmersham Park in 1813 'amuse themselves very comfortably in the even'g – by netting; they are each about a rabbit net'.

Most netting projects were purses of various kinds, so much so that netting boxes were frequently referred to as 'purse-netting boxes'. Such boxes would also contain moulds shaped like rounded, hollow, wooden cups that were used to form the net into the purse shape correctly. Thousands of socking purses were made. The long, slender shape also became known as a 'miser's purse' because of its meagre centre aperture closed with metal sliders. Towards the end of the eighteenth century the stocking purse became long enough to fall elegantly to both sides when held in the hand or, at up to 17 inches long, to be looped over a belt. The ends would usually be decorated differently with tassels or fringes so that it was easy to open it to the correct end depending on which coins were required. In London there were specialist shops, such as Thomas Gardom of St James' Street, to supply 'purse twist, tassels and sliders of all sorts', but elsewhere the resources of haberdasher or milliner had to be relied upon.

In *Pride and Prejudice* Mr Bingley was impressed by those ladies who would 'paint tables, cover skreens and net purses', while inevitably Mr Darcy was scathing that the term 'accomplished' should be applied to 'many a woman who deserves it no otherwise than by netting a purse of covering a skreen'. Darcy was not the only gentleman left cold

'The Western Exchange on Old Bond Street' by G. Smith, 1817. Like other nineteenth-century bazaars it was full of individual sellers offering haberdashery, trimmings and glamourous accessories, but, being close to the fashionable tailors of Jermyn Street, it was particularly renowned for male accessories.

by the vogue of netting purses, which were often made in green silk – the colour of true love – to be presented as a love token. In one of their many letters during the 1790s Lord Bessborough entreated Sarah Ponsonby: 'I desire the favour of you not to send me the Purse you mention, for I have, I believe, twenty by me which are not of any use. It has been the fashion of ladies to make purses and they have been so obliging as to give me a great many.'

Knotting

Using a similar shuttle with silk, cotton or wool threads, 'notting' was a craft related to netting. Creating artful knots in a thread like a string of beads, these could be couched into embroideries to add interest and texture or made into short lengths for fringing. As a boy Jane's nephew Frank enjoyed 'notting yards of fringing' for curtains, a hobby shared by Lady Bertram in *Mansfield Park*.

It was not always easy to get the materials and trim required, so frequently when a relative was going to London or a fashionable town such as Bath, they would be besieged with requests for materials, trimmings and haberdashery. Jane wrote from Steventon in October 1798 that at Mrs Ryder's shop there was 'scarcely any notting silk; but Miss Wood as usual, is going to town very soon, & will lay in a fresh stock'. Seemingly none was available as a few months later she writes, 'I am still without silk. You must get me some in town or in Canterbury,' adding with characteristic mischievous wit, 'It should be finer than yours.'

The natural antecedent to the reticule was the knotting bag, which, ostensibly to carry the accoutrements for the fashionable hobby, became something of a display item in the 1790s. It provided a pretty showcase for the ladies' knotting and needlework talents, which Mr Bingley in *Pride and Prejudice* considered a great female accomplishment, and, as Lady Mary Coke noted as early as 1769, 'She had a knotting-bag, embroidered, hanging to her arm – "tho indeed," said she "I never knott, but the bag is convenient for one's gloves and Fan".'

Tambouring and Embroidery

With the popularity of muslin came a vogue for doing tambour work or embroidery where the fabric was mounted drum-tight on a frame to be worked with a fine hook-ended needle. From 1785 the *Ladies' Domestic Magazine* offered all manner of lovely designs that could be drawn onto the delicate muslin fabric once placed on the tambour frame to be embroidered white on white with silk thread. Designs varied from a simple spots or floral motifs, such as the shawl Jane made, which is on display at her Hampshire home, to sophisticated neoclassical designs inspired by the latest discoveries of the ancient world.

Like Catherine Morland's tamboured muslin gown in *Northanger Abbey*, many yards of muslin were tamboured and silk, gauze and tulle embroidered to create a gown, or rather the length of fabric required to be sent to a dressmaker to be made up to the desired design. Frequently the pattern would be taken from an existing gown – probably made by the same

'Morning Employments', George Morland (*c.* 1794). Gathering round the tambouring frame, the circular frame mounted on a stand allowed the embroiderer to accomplish large areas of simple stitch while seated elegantly in company. Mrs Grant has a tambour frame in *Mansfield Park* from where she likes to play matchmaker.

Embroidery pattern from *Ackermann's Repository of Arts* (1 April 1816). These well-proportioned designs appeared in magazines throughout the period. They could be traced onto muslin to be embroidered white on white for fashion, or a more robust backing to be completed in colour as part of an interior-design project.

dressmaker – to ensure a good fit. A local dressmaker would be adequate for most needs, with superior items to be purchased on visits to London or Bath.

Fashion

Since the advent of Nicolaus Heideloff's magazine *The Gallery of Fashion* in 1794 the fashion press had become a phenomenon. Each month brought beautiful new fashion plates to entice and inspire the reader to have the latest styles made up, to makeover her existing wardrobe or to begin planning how she could make her own glorious accessories.

Some fashion magazines were published in two versions, La Belle Assemblée offered a more expensive version where all the plates were hand-coloured, and a more basic version where the plates remained undecorated. Ladies and more prestigious dressmakers subscribed to receive the full version, whereas for only a few pence the less expensive version was widely accessible to more middle-class women.

Women in the countryside, further away from the fashionable cities, had to wait longer for their fashion intelligence. Before the penny post the Royal Mail was expensive, relying on coaches to deliver mail, and it would take days, possibly weeks, for information to travel any distance. Women who participated in London society or who visited the fashionable

'Messrs Harding Howell & Co, 89 Pall Mall' from *Ackermann's Repository of Arts* (1809), which asserted that 'for the last twelve years by the present proprietors, who have spared neither trouble nor expence to ensure the establishment a superiority over every other in Europe, and to render it perfectly unique in its kind'.

October, 1809.—Vol. 2.

The Repository

Of Arts, Literature, Commerce, Manufactures, Fashions, and Politics.

MANUFACTURERS, Factors, and Wholesale Dealers in Fancy Goods, that come within the scope of this Plan, are requested to send Patterns of such new Articles, as they come out; and if the requisites of Novelty, Fashion, and Elegance, are united, the quantity necessary for this Magazine will be ordered.

R. Ackermann, 101, Strand, London.

Left: 'Allegorical Woodcut with Patterns of British Manufacture', *Ackermann's Repository of Arts* (October 1809). The magazine regularly included small fabric swatches with descriptions and recommendations for their use; for example, No. 4, 'a rose-coloured book muslin, best calculated for the ball-room or evening party.'

Below: 'English Mannequin' (*c.* 1800). Fashion paper dolls with costumes to cut out became increasingly popular during the 1790s when *The English Doll,* an 8-inch paper doll with an envelope full of the latest fashions, was the favoured way to convey fashion news to America.

'Morning Dress' invented by Mrs Bell, engraved for No. 72 of *La Belle Assemblée* (1 July 1815). Wearing a typically warm, informal indoor morning dress made stylish with the additions of a cap with elegant plumes and pink roses with pink satin slippers, she pores over a fashion magazine during breakfast.

centres were prevailed upon to relay every scrap of detail about the outfits of the most fashionable ladies they had seen, like Mrs Gardiner in *Pride and Prejudice*, whose first duty upon arriving at the Bennets' was to 'distribute her presents and describe the latest fashions'. They were undoubtedly pleased to do so with a sense of one-upmanship too, but probably only after they had already commissioned their own dressmakers to start work!

Jane Austen herself regularly included fashion news in her letters when she was in Bath or London: 'I am amused by the present style of female dress; - the coloured petticoats with braces over the white Spencers & enormous Bonnets upon the full stretch, are quite entertaining. It seems to me a more marked change than one has lately seen.'

The magazines were pored over and passed on throughout family and friendship groups, with the designs copied, adapted or simply coloured in. *Ackermann's Repository* had a wide range of watercolours available for the amateur artist, and this season's fashionable colours were always included for those who enjoyed decorating their fashion plates.

During the Regency era fashions started to change more rapidly, and for women like Jane who did not have a large disposable income the ability to alter and trim gowns and make her own accessories was essential. With the rise of the fashion press compelling style to change not only season by season but month by month, one of the best ways to keep up was to make accessories to emulate those featured. Only the biggest and most fashionable towns like London and Bath had a decent selection of shops, but they all had a haberdasher or milliner who could supply a dazzling array of ribbons, feathers, buttons and buckles.

Above left: 'Walking Dress' from *Ackermann's Repository of Arts August* (1814). 'A lilac sarsnet petticoat, full flounce round the bottom, confined by plaits or tufts of ribband of corresponding colour ... high plain body of white sarsnet buttoned behind; long full sleeve with lace ruffle and full lace ruff. Lilac scarf sash worn in braces and tied behind in bows and ends. A Russian bonnet lilac kid sandals and gloves.'

Above right: 'A Visit to the Milliners', a fashion plate from the German magazine *Neues Journal Fur Fabriken, Manufakturen, Handlung, Kunst und Mode*, April 1809.. Both Jane and Cassandra took great pleasure in decorating caps.

A vogue for artificial flowers and fruits appeared in the late 1790s. In a letter to Cassandra, Jane wrote:

Flowers are very much worn, & Fruit is still more the thing. – Elizth has a bunch of Strawberries, & I have seen Grapes, cherries, Plumbs, & Apricots – There are likewise Almonds & raisins, French plumbs & Tamarinds at the Grocers, but I have never seen any of them in hats' in her next letter she adds 'besides I cannot help thinking that it is more natural to have flowers grow out of the head than fruit.

In December 1798, when Jane is deeply involved in making a new cap, she writes to Cassandra:

I took the liberty a few days ago of asking your black velvet bonnet to lend me its cawl, which it very readily did, and by which I have been enabled to give a considerable improvement of dignity to my cap, which was before too nidgetty to please me. I shall wear it on Thursday, but I hope you will not be offended with me for following your advice as to its ornaments only in part. I still venture to retain the narrow silver round it, Put twice round without any bow, and instead of the black military feather shall put in the Coquelicot one, as being smarter; and besides Coquelicot is to be all the fashion this winter. After the ball, I shall probably make it entirely black...

Shoemaking

Shoemaking also became a popular pastime, as the Hon. Mrs Calvert noted in her *Souvenirs* for 1808: 'There was hardly a lady's work table that was not covered in shoemaker's tools ... I begin a new science today – shoemaking. It is all the fashion. I had a master with me for two hours.' Whereas Jane wrote to her niece Anna in 1814: 'Your Grandmamma desires me to say that she will have finished your Shoes tomorrow & thinks they will look very well.' It was not necessarily the whole shoe that was constructed; more often just the vamp was embroidered to create the prettiest dancing slippers to match a favourite gown.

Painting at Home

Where watercolour landscapes were one of the best ways to record the mood of a picturesque scene or a rosy-tinged sunset, the amateur artist did more serious work at home. In *Emma*, our heroine applies greater effort to painting Harriet Smith's portrait than any of her previous works, with all, despite their merits, left forgotten and unfinished. This portrait holds more interest because it is pivotal to her scheme to make a match between Harriet and Mr Elton, but the fact that it reflects the makeover she has already undertaken on Harriet's personality and that it garners fawning praise might also have maintained her interest.

At the opening of the era artists still had to visit the apothecary to purchase pigments they would have to mix by hand. In 1781 the first great innovation for artists was made by the Reeves brothers, Thomas and William, who were awarded a silver palette by the Society of Arts for their improved watercolour paints. With the success of his drawing books, it was natural for Rudolph Ackermann to also manufacture his own range of artists' paints and papers.

He promoted his innovations with his *A Treatise on Ackermann's Superfine Watercolours* (1801) when he had extended his range to sixty-nine colours, including his own chemical compositions for white and yellow, as well as Ackermann's Green and Ackermann's Brown, both of which feature repeatedly in his fashion plates from the Repository. This along with the presentation of the colours in beautiful paintboxes of mahogany, yew or satinwood, complete with a marble tray and a saucer for mixing made them most desirable. His ad in 1810 claimed they were sold at 'all Booksellers, Printsellers and Stationers in Great Britain,' along with a wide range of Ackerman's prints and publications.

Ackermann's coloured plates, transparencies and fancy papers were also essential for home crafts for découpage to make fire screens and to line and decorate boxes.

Mlle Charlotte du Val D'ognes or 'Young Woman Drawing' (1801). This enigmatic portrait, perhaps self-portrait, was once attributed to Jacques Louis David, but is now accepted as being by Marie Denice Villers. The artist observes intensely, working alone, while beyond the broken window a frivolous happy couple stroll together.

5

Masculine Pleasures

Used to the impressive military display of the era, male fashion held equal importance to female, with the dandiest displays taking place at the racecourse. Horsepower and speed were as important to the Regency gentleman as they are to the modern petrolhead, and both horse racing and the latest carriage designs were a constant talking point. Such was the passion for speed that gentlemen would offer handsome tips to the drivers of stagecoaches for a chance to 'take the ribbons'.

'Jerry in Training for A Swell' from *Life in London* by Pierce Egan (1822). The tailor's art could make anyone a fine figure of a gentleman, even if – like the one discarded on the floor – a corset were required.

Gambling was a perpetual pastime at the racetrack, card table and gentlemen's clubs, frequently with such high stakes that entire family estates were lost in a single evening. Even though wagers were formed over all manner of things, they were always taken very seriously and any accusation of cheating was greeted with a demand for satisfaction to be settled with a duel.

The traditional country pursuits of riding, hunting and fishing saw renewed popularity and a range of new styles loosely inspired by Beau Brummel reinvigorated an interest in fashion.

Throughout the eighteenth century European opinion was that the English were a nation who always took things to extremes, and with gambling it couldn't be more true. Just as the Volstead Act calling for prohibition inspired a cult for cocktails in the 1930s, the Gambling Act of 1739 seemed to more than encourage gambling by providing a daring frisson of the illicit. It also provided the opportunity for additional crimes. Deals were done whereby for a share of the winnings, footpads and highwaymen would be tipped off so that a winner could be relieved of his haul on the way home. Those who lost were extorted by creditors or loan sharks, and once gambling was illegal there was the ever-ready threat of blackmail.

Gaming had long been popular, but once driven underground the stakes became infinitely higher and entire estates were lost at the turn of a card. As Dr Johnson observed in his dictionary, there was a marked difference between gaming and the extravagantly high stakes of gambling.

Those with little to lose would regularly risk life and limb, but even the elegant, privileged young gentlemen at White's Club salved their ennui with ridiculous wagers. Beau Brummel was among them, often gambling so outrageously that eventually he had to flee to France to evade his creditors.

Socialite hostesses forged dubious reputations and large fortunes by operating gambling salons, frequently with the strong-armed assistance of rather less-than-gentlemanly enforcers.

'Tattersall's Horse Repository' by A. C. Pugin and J. Bluck from Ackermann's *Microcosm of London* (1808). Stylish gentlemen would spend a fortune on elegant equestrian accoutrements.

An unusual fashion plate depicting a lady gambling from *Journal des Dames et des Modes, Costume Parisien* (Plate 1,407, An. 10 of the French Revolution – 1802). She is wearing a *tunique á la mameluck* and calculating her winnings, represented by the mother of pearl gaming counters on the table. These were often in the shape of fish, as in *Pride and Prejudice*: 'Lydia talked incessantly of the fish she had lost and the fish she had won.'

The notorious Lady Archer hosted a salon, and she was not averse to participating in races and feats of daring for the sake of gambling opportunities.

There was a worrying link between gambling and sex, the suggestion being that if a young lady were seduced by the thrill of gambling she might be susceptible to other temptations. Unfortunately, the grim reality was more that some male players would deliberately target pretty neophyte gamblers and insist that their debts were paid in very personal favours. There were also husbands so disgraceful that they would wager the favours of their wives, mistresses or even their children to repay their debts. It is no great surprise then that gambling could also be damaging to feminine beauty, as was noted in *The Spectator*:

There is nothing that wears out a fine Face like the Vigils of the Card Table, and those cutting Passions which naturally attend them. Hollow Eyes, haggard Looks, and pale Complexions, are the natural Indications of a Female Gamester. Her Morning Sleeps are not able to repair her Midnight Watchings. I have known a Woman carried off half dead from Basette, and have, many a time grieved to see a Person of Quality gliding by me, in her Chair, at two a Clock in the Morning, and looking like a Spectre amid a flare of Flambeaux. In short, I never knew a thorough paced Female Gamester hold her Beauty two Winters together.

In 1797 Lord Kenyon threatened to make an example of upper-class gamblers who thought that they were 'too great for the law', adding, 'I wish they could be punished ... if any prosecutions of this kind are fairly brought before me, and the parties are justly convicted, whatever be their rank or station in the country, though they be the first ladies in the land, they shall certainly exhibit themselves in the pillory.'

It seems that he was as good as his word, as James Gilray's satirical drawing *Faro's Daughters Beware* (1797) depicts Lady Buckinghamshire tied to the tail of a cart being flogged by Kenyon, while Lady Luttrell and Mrs Sturt look on from their position in the pillory.

Gambling became far less popular, with it changing context at the end of the century. Where once it had been a necessary salve for the boredom and ennui of an unproductive existence, with the upheavals of the French Revolution felt keenly across the aristocratic classes and the consequent call to war, priorities were suddenly changed. Undoubtedly, many idle hours were spent gambling while the various army and navy regiments awaited orders, but the feverish society-wide compulsion to gamble died once more important concerns were at hand.

The outside was the male domain: one of land ownership, work and potential, whether it was potential adventure or potential danger, potential artistic garden design or potential enterprise. A lady was very much confined within the grounds of her home unless someone could go with her. To venture abroad alone was to risk being frightened by gypsies as Harriet was in *Emma*, or twisting an ankle like Marianne in *Sense and Sensibility* from which she would have to be rescued.

Masculine pleasures were usually kept out of the sphere of feminine experience. It was considered a little uncouth to spend too much time talking about hunting and shooting

'The Hunter' by Henry Thomas Alken, from Alken's *The National Sports of Great Britain* (first published in 1821). Hunting and shooting were popular and prestigious pastimes only accessible to the highest echelons of society, and a capable horse was a valuable status symbol.

'Ladies Riding Dress', *La Belle Assemblée* (1 June 1812). Equestrian, curricle or walking costume: 'A habit of bright green ornamented down the front and embroidered at the cuffs à la militaire with black. Small riding hat of black beaver fancifully adorned with gold cordon and tassels, with a long ostrich feather of green in the front; or a green hat with black tassels and black feather.'

in mixed company because it was a little distasteful and more than a little dull. Jane uses an over interest in hunting and shooting as an indicator of a shallow personality. Darcy will hunt and shoot but as part of managing his estate or providing entertainment for his guests, whereas Sir John Middleton is identified as rather gauche because it is his primary measure of all things.

There were strict rules for the hunting and shooting of game to exclude those, as the law put it, 'persons of mean estates' whose estates yielded an income of less than £100 per annum. After 1784 a game certificate costing 3 guineas was also required and the proper rules had to be adhered to – keeping to the hunting season and never hunting at night on Sunday or on Christmas day. Hunting hare was most popular, as the number of deer was already in decline with the reduction of forests and fox hunting was not to become fully popular until the Victorian era. Hare were hunted by men on horseback with packs of harrier hounds for 'sport', but it was forbidden to hunt them with snares or by tracking them in the snow.

The shooting of game birds made a major contribution to the household by way of larder and dining table. In *Emma*, Mr Knightly, as a responsible gentleman, uses his estate to provide food and entertainment for the neighbourhood rather than solitary sport for himself. Whereas **eto** *Sense and Sensibility* the inveterate sportsman Sir John Middleton, in his generosity in providing a cottage to home Mrs Dashwood and her daughters, is also ensuring that the feminine household will harbour no rival hunters. Jane writes:

In shewing kindness to his cousins … he had the real satisfaction of a good heart; and in settling a family of females only in his cottage, he had all the satisfaction of a sportsman; for a sportsman though he esteems only those of his sex who are sportsmen likewise, is not often desirous of encouraging their taste by admitting them to a residence within his own manor.

Willoughby is introduced with the overtly masculine image of the consummate sportsman, if not predator: 'A gentleman carrying a gun, with two pointers playing round him was passing up the hill.' He is out alone shooting when he meets Marianne, and although he rescues her, he also sees her vulnerability and ensnares her. He has his own 'pretty little estate in Somersetshire,' Sir John informs us, yet he is making use of those of his elderly female cousin as though they were already his own, testing the merits of the land before he inherits. This uneasy image defines him and heralds the destruction wrought by his predatory nature later in the novel.

There was plenty of advice for the would-be sportsman via the wide selection of instruction manuals published during the era, as well, undoubtedly, from almost every older gentleman who wanted to relate his tall tales as much as to impart knowledge.

The Revolutionary and Napoleonic Wars had taken their toll and created a restlessness for those not adequately involved. They required other thrills to fill long, idle days and inevitably stave off thoughts of lost brothers and friends.

Pleasures were in many ways related to military life. Pugilism took over from warfare, gambling took over from daring, and fine horses, fine fashion and hard living took over the rest. At a time of social instability and the extension of polite society, the 'ton' – the fashionable elite – were determinedly exclusive, codifying minute divisions daily to ensure that they were impossible to truly emulate.

The finest dandy and undisputed head of the ton, Beau Brummell, was close friend and keen influence on the Prince Regent. The ton were the all-important arbiters of taste. Dominating London's social season, they defined the fashionable world, which mostly fell between Pall Mall, Piccadilly, St James' Street and St James' Square.

Portrait of George 'Beau' Brummell, c. 1805. Beau Brummell used subtle style to frame his ego with an arrogant insouciance, which was doggedly emulated by his followers including his 'fat friend', the Prince Regent.

White's was *the* club of the Regency era – if you made White's you were truly in. But, as one contemporary noted, it was '*the* club from which people died of exclusion … killed on the spot by a black ball; *the* club where in dandy existence, either you must live or you have no life'. Even then there was an inner circle centred around Beau Brummell, who presided over and passed judgement on the fashionable world from the vantage point of the bow window overlooking St James' Street. This space for the 'Unique Four' – Beau Brummell, Lord Alvanley, Sir Henry Mildmay and Henry Pierrepoint – was sacrosanct and no other member would presume to sit there.

Brooks's, the Whig stronghold, and Boodles were almost on a par, but founded in 1807 by the Prince of Wales's chef, Waiter's soon came to rival White's as the 'great-go'. It was also favoured by the dandies and notorious for fortunes lost in high-stakes card games such as faro and hazard, but it had the distinction of serving excellent food.

There was a strong sense of national identity and what a good Englishman should demonstrate, and indeed prove himself to be. He should be keen to test his courage, demonstrate his prowess and be ready to step into the fray to defend honour, family, king and country, and yet he should do it all with an affable sense of fair play. In peacetime sport was lauded as the forum in which to make such displays. This fashionable corner of London also housed many of the key venues beloved of the 'Corinthian', a sort of sporting dandy subgroup whose tastes may have been a little too brash with bright, striped waistcoats and overly tall hats, but they were no less gentlemen.

Once he had won the title of English champion from Mendoza in 1795, John 'Gentleman' Jackson set up a boxing school for gentlemen in nearby Bond Street. Places were coveted and even the most aristocratic gentlemen had to be properly introduced before they could apply for lessons. In his landmark 1813 volume *Boxiana*, Pierce Egan declares: 'Boxing came from Nature! Wounded feelings brought manly resentment to its aid – and coolness,

'The Great Subscription Room at Brooks's Club' by A. C. Pugin and J. Bluck from Ackermann's *Microcosm of London* (1808). Although primarily a political club, Brooks's kept their membership to an exclusive 450 nominated members at a subscription of 11 guineas a year.

Fashion Plate 1,237 from *Journal des Dames et des Modes Costume Parisien* (1812). He wears the striped waistcoat of a sporting gentleman 'Corinthian' along with a dashing stylishly cut redingote, and trousers, or *pantalon*, of practical hardwearing nankeen.

checking fiery passion and rage, reduced it to a perfect science.' Thereby, he summoned a view of pugilism as a kind of rational heroism, which was infinitely appealing to those who sought views of enlightened philosophy and romantic sensibilities.

Taught self-defence by Gentleman Jackson, Lord Byron was a devotee, but James Beresford suggested that allowing 'a great raw-boned fellow to thrash you 3-4 times a week because you may some time or other, have a fancy to thrash someone else' was one of miseries in his 1807 satirical title *The Miseries of Human Life*.

Despite being illegal, boxing was also a great spectator sport, attracting a considerable following. Magistrates usually turned a blind eye as 'the fancy', or fans of boxing, included the Prince Regent, for whom, with his royal guests, Lord Lowther organised fights between some of the most celebrated boxers at his home in Pall Mall in June 1814.

Prize fights were usually organised beyond the limits of city or town, with the precise location kept a well-guarded secret until the eleventh hour. Despite the great inconvenience of organising last-minute travel, disappointing English weather and the risks of attending such an event beyond the law, huge crowds attended. Pierce Egan reported on the fight between Jack Scroggins and Ned Turner on 26 May 1817 in a field near Hayes that 'there were not less than 30,000 persons present' and the crush was so great that the ring was broken, the ropes trampled underfoot, and even when the organisers wielded their horsewhips to force the crowds back they could not gain enough space for the fight to continue. Having each paid 3s, there were a few additional fights before the crowd was dispersed, many choosing to continue in the pelting rain to Arlington Corner, near Hounslow Heath, to see at least one fight before the day was over.

It would appear that as boxing grew in appeal, becoming a national sport, it also gained female followers. In October 1816 Egan reports on a fight at Gretna Green, saying that on

'The Art of Self Defence' taught at John 'Gentleman' Jackson's boxing school, from *Life in London* by Pierce Egan (1822). Gentlemen are boxing and fencing, while another is being weighed for the sake of a wager.

the day of the fight 'all the houses in Carlisle and its vicinity were totally drained of the male population – females only were left to conduct business...' However, in May 1823, for a fight at Hinckley Down in Hampshire, there were upwards of 30,000 spectators 'among them numerous well-dressed females'.

After beating the American champion Tom Molyneux in 1811, the famous English boxing champion Tom Cribb bought the King's Arms tavern and opened Cribb's Parlour – perhaps the first sports bar – to display his own memorabilia and to act as a hub for fighters and Corinthians to discuss matters of pugilism and sport while also learning the secret location of the next fight.

Tattersall's was also within convenient strutting distance from White's. Essentially an auction house for horses, Tattersall had established such a reputation for knowledge and integrity that his sale yard near Hyde Park Corner became an institution and the only place to buy a thoroughbred. There was stabling for 100 horses plus kennels and everything from racehorse to coach horse, hunter and hounds were available at weekly auctions, as was an excellent selection of tack and harnesses. It was a popular pastime for gentlemen to take a stroll around Tattersall's and stopping in the elegantly pillared courtyard to view the parade of horses before retiring to the fine subscription room where, for an annual fee of a guinea, gentlemen could socialise and lay bets on racing and other sporting events. All winnings were paid and debts settled promptly on Mondays – without exception.

Gambling was everywhere at all kinds of sporting events, especially racing and boxing, but also at ghastly, cruel sports such as dog or cockfighting. The Westminster Pit specialised in such horrors, most famously Billy a 'bull and terrier'. It was reported in *The Sporting Magazine* in October 1822 that Billy was able to kill 100 rats in less than six minutes, far exceeding the expectations of most who bet on him. In *Life in London* Pierce Egan also relates the appalling fight between 'that extraordinary and celebrated creature, The famed Italian monkey of Hoxton, Jacco Maccacco and a dog of 20lbs weight, the property of a Nobleman well-known in the circle.' Possibly some kind of gibbon or baboon, of around

'Cribb's Parlour' from *Life in London* by Pierce Egan (1822) where you could meet the pugilistic hero in person, see his trophies, and discuss sport and the latest sporting wagers.

'Jacco Maccacco at the Westminster Pit' from *Life in London* by Pierce Egan (1822). The audience proclaimed the poor monkey as they would a prize fighter, and there was a purse of 100 guineas (£6,400 approximately) on this obscene fight.

just 10 lbs, was brought into the pit in a 'little wooden house'. Once removed, he had a narrow chain placed around his middle and attached to a post so he could not escape into the crowd, who stood pressed together regardless of class and calling – chimney sweep jockeying with MP, all desperate to see if their bet would win. Jacco quickly dispatched the dog as he had been rumoured to have killed his previous fourteen 'opponents' and three of his previous owners' fingers. The following year he was pitted against the boxer Tom Cribb's dog Puss. This event was cited in a speech at the House of Commons in 1822 pushing for legislation against animal cruelty, which contributed to the Metropolis Act of 1822 making it illegal to keep or use a baiting arena within 5 miles of Temple Bar. There had been calls against animal cruelty and cruel sports since the 1740s but to little avail. A parliamentary debate in 1800 was dismissed by William Windham, Secretary of War, saying that, 'It is beneath the dignity of the legislature to interfere with matters of such a frivolous nature ... [and try to] curtail the amusements of the lower orders.' His argument being that if baiting of bulls and other animals was banned then legislation against hunting and shooting would inevitably follow.

The dandies at White's would bet on anything. There was even one notorious case in 1816 when Beau Brummel's pal Lord Alvanley bet £3,000 on the progress of two raindrops running down the bow window at White's. At the club all the bets were carefully logged in leather-bound volumes. At first this was the duty of servants, but by Brummell's day the responsibility passed to the members. This was marked by some wag who wrote in the margin: 'About this time it is supposed the nobility of England began to learn to write.'

Despite their frivolous nature the bets were taken very seriously, and gambling debts were taken as a matter of honour, even though (unfortunately for many business owners, especially tailors) other debts were largely ignored sometimes for years. It might be possible to buy some time by issuing a vowel – an IOU – but usually it was a matter of honour to settle a gambling debt quickly.

It was one thing to lose to friends, fellow club members and fellow gentlemen, but near to the elite clubs there were more than a few 'gambling hells' in St James', where the action was far more cut-throat.

The idea of losing face or being dishonoured in front of others within his social milieu was unconscionable for a gentleman, and any suggestion that he had failed to settle a gambling debt adequately was enough to provoke a challenge to a duel. Insulting someone's integrity was also grounds, as was physical attack, but by far the most common grounds for throwing down the gauntlet was to dishonour or attempt to take advantage of a lady.

If there were grounds for a challenge it had to be issued, and once issued it had to be seen through by both parties. Beau Brummell once managed to use self-deprecating humour to diffuse a challenge.

Generally speaking, gentlemen had to be prepared, and to do so they could take lessons in fencing from instructors such as Henry Angelo in Bond Street, whose pupils were some of the most illustrious gentlemen of the era, so much so that his volume of *Reminiscences*

'Untimely Irruption of the Police into a Fashionable Gaming House' published by Thomas Kelly (12 January 1822). Gambling hells were notorious for duping young, inexperienced players with their loaded dice, known as 'Fulhams', and were frequently raided.

(1828) was a bestseller. Lord Byron was a pupil as much for fitness and to deal with his weight problem as to deal with any challenge.

Duels by sword had fallen from favour since the 1780s and, paradoxically, duels by pistols were safer and far less likely to result in fatality. Joseph Manton made the most beautiful flintlock pistols in perfectly matched pairs for duelling. In order that gentlemen could gain full benefit of these coveted status symbols, Manton also ran a shooting gallery in nearby Davies Street where they could practice to improve their marksmanship skills. There, wafer papers were attached to 3-foot-wide, cast-iron targets to be shot at from a distance of 15 yards. A good shot would be able to 'culp' twelve wafers within six minutes, including having to reload between each shot. Anything better would be considered excellent marksmanship, and such crack shot were rarely challenged.

There were a few women who were expert with pistols but they were inevitably limited to practising at home in private with whatever weapons their family possessed.

A duel is referenced in *Sense and Sensibility*, but only obliquely. Jane thereby reflects Colonel Brandon's distaste in being forced to engage in such a vile task and allows for the duel to be echoed in the counter and parry of Brandon and Willoughby's confidences to Elinor.

Colonel Brandon explains to Elinor that he had an 'unavoidable' meeting with Willoughby: '[We] met by appointment, he to defend, I to punish his conduct,' as the seducer of Eliza, his ward. 'Have you,' she continued, after a short silence, 'ever seen Mr Willoughby since you left him at Barton?' 'Yes,' he replied gravely, 'once I have. One meeting was unavoidable.' Elinor, startled by his manner, looked at him anxiously, saying, 'What? have you met him to—' 'I could meet him in no other way. Eliza had confessed to me, though most reluctantly, the name of her lover; and when he returned to town, which was within a fortnight after myself, we met by appointment, he to defend, I to punish his

'The Fortunate Duellist', a satirical print of Captain James Macrae (1790), depicting him practising his aim at a barber's block mounted on a pole.

conduct. We returned unwounded, and the meeting, therefore, never got abroad.' Elinor sighed over the fancied necessity of this; but to a man and a soldier, she presumed not to censure it.

One notorious duel that Jane may well have been aware of is that of the fortunate duellist, Captain James Macrae. On 7 April 7 1790 at the Theatre Royal in Edinburgh he was forced to chastise a footman who insulted him. Despite that fact that the 'chastisement' was quite a severe beating, the matter was considered closed once apologies were exchanged between Macrae and the servant's employers, Sir George and Lady Ramsay. However, the footman James Merry, in an unprecedented move, took matters into his own hands and issued a summons on 12 April against Captain Macrae. With the fear of revolution burgeoning on this side of the Channel, barely nine months since the Bastille had been stormed, such a challenge against traditional roles and class privilege was deeply troubling to Edinburgh society and a humiliating affront to Macrae, his rank and his class.

The following day Macrae issued a demand for satisfaction to Sir George Ramsay stating that he must force the footman to withdraw the charges against him or 'turn him off' if he would not. Outraged at being told what to do, or being named a scoundrel if he would not, Sir George took Macrae's demand as a challenge and a duel was set for noon on Wednesday 14 April 1790.

Captain Macrae was well known to diligently practice his duelling skills by shooting at a barber's block set up in his garden, and had earned a reputation as a fearsome and dangerous duellist. His reputation was amply proven as the duel resulted in Sir George being mortally wounded. He died on 16 April, by which time Macrae had fled to France. He remained there for the rest of his life, unable to return because, although the law might turn a blind eye to gentlemen duelling to settle their quarrels, the resulting death carried a charge of murder.

6

Romantic Pleasures

Romance leading to a successful engagement is the supreme goal that lies at the heart of all Jane Austen's works as it was a key concern for most families. The daughters of the nobility and gentry were entirely the hostages of fortune on the 'marriage market' and it was absolutely vital to make a good match for the sake of ensuring a reasonable future. Property was only ever transferred through the male line, so to avoid being plunged into homelessness and poverty like the Dashwoods at the opening of *Sense and Sensibility*, it

'Musical Entertainments' (*c.* 1800), contemporary watercolour by unknown artist. Under the watchful eye of her stout mother the harpist plays to impress their swaggering military guests while her sisters barely conceal their boredom.

was essential to make a good marriage. The choice of husband was greatly curtailed by family interests and opinions. The cooing over Mr Darcy's £10,000 a year is underlined by the stark reality that, with no other prospects, a girl had to marry well enough to secure not only her own future, but that of her mother and unmarried sisters. Critics of Austen often cite the preoccupation with making a good marriage match in her novels as evidence of trivial, frivolous concerns rather than engaging with the issues of the day, but to Jane and the generations of women like her it was fundamental to their survival.

Romance still held every frivolous pleasure, but it was draped over an underlying strategy that the Duke of Wellington himself would consider well played. From the cradle young ladies were groomed to be charming and pleasant with little regard to their own feelings, no doubt so they were used to being subservient to their husband's needs. Their accomplishments were so that they could provide musical entertainment, stimulating conversation or attractive decor items to grace their husband's home. While, most importantly, their looks should be fresh and pretty enough to earn a husband compliments, they should not be too obvious as to gain individual attention for her.

It was also a lifelong commitment for parents to network, develop their connections and enhance their PROGRESS best place to be seen and hopefully introduced to a potential partner. It was not just a pleasure to hold a glamourous ball for all the important families of the county, it was a social obligation to provide opportunities for people to socialise and for the younger generation to develop their social graces and foster relationships. When Mr Bingley arrives at Netherfield the first thing he does is to organise a ball, allowing him

'Evening or Full Dress', *Ackermann's Repository of Arts* (June 1810). Sharing a moment swooning over a portrait miniature of a beloved beau, she wears a round robe of white gossamer satin over pink satin with a lace ruffle at neckline and cuff, with gloves and Roman slippers of white kid and a carved ivory fan. Her companion wears white crape over blue sarsnet with a border of blue roses and white satin shoes.

Above left: 'Evening Full Dresses', *La Belle Assemblée* (1 March 1810). A white satin round dress with half-yard train laced up the back and seams with a gold twist, ornamented around the pointed neckline with a twill of frosted satin, with an Emsdorf helmet. The pianist wears the same cut of bodice in green velvet, but her skirt is of white satin with an Indian muslin over skirt and train. Both headdresses are completed with craped ostrich feathers and a Theresa curl over the left shoulder.

Above right: 'Ball Dress', *Ackermann's Repository of Arts* (1 June 1813). Described as 'evening or ball dress, a Grecian robe of lilac or apple-blossom crape worn over a white satin petticoat. A satin bodice ornamented with white beads à *la militaire*. With bold 'Indian turban of silver frosted crape' and 'fan of ivory decorated with coloured feathers' as well as a green 'scarf' embroidered in gold – no one could remain a wallflower wearing this!

to make a super first impression as a socially responsible gentleman, as well as giving him an opportunity to meet everyone important and eligible.

Social obligation extended beyond providing entertainment. The reason why Lizzie forms such a poor initial impression of Darcy is because he is ungallantly refusing to dance while there are young ladies in desperate need of partners being forced to become wallflowers. It was acceptable for ladies to stand up together to dance – and Jane does at the Basingstoke assembly – but it was far from desirable and more suited to ladies who are a little more mature. Jane wrote to Cassandra in November 1800:

It was a pleasant ball, and still more good than pleasant, for there were nearly sixty people, and sometimes we had seventeen couples... There was a scarcity of men in general, and a still greater scarcity of any that were good for much. I danced nine dances out of ten – five with Stephen Terry, T. Chute, and James Digweed, and four with Catherine. There was commonly a couple of ladies standing up together, but not often any so amiable as ourselves.

The ability to dance well was crucial, as it could make all the difference as to whether a desired invitation was forthcoming. The prestigious subscription balls held each week of the season at Almack's were the best possible point of display for a debutante, as the formidable patronesses who organised the events maintained the highest possible standards at the club. Competition was fierce for the vouchers to attend the balls, and selection was frequently made according to who would be as asset on the dance floor. Beau Brummel heightened his young reputation by dancing well and being perpetually chosen. In his memoirs Captain Gronow relates how Lady Jersey invited a guards officer who was a delightful dancer, but excluded his wife because she wasn't. So incensed by the snub and the upset it caused his wife, the officer challenged Lord Jersey to a duel.

Throughout the eighteenth century the delicate movements of the minuet were so closely related to the refined and graceful deportment of the aristocratic classes that it seemed remiss to need instruction. It was Georgiana Duchess of Devonshire who first broke this unwritten rule in 1779 when she organised dance classes for a group of young ladies to help with the new up-tempo dances.

The minuet was still taught in Jane Austen's day as a foundation for dance, deportment and ballroom etiquette. Such instruction would come from a visiting dancing master who would teach a group from several local families together so costs could be shared and a wealth of partners provided. There were also children's balls so they were familiar with the ballroom before having to make their first official appearance.

Jane was taught her first steps by her mother and brothers at Steventon, but those with smaller incomes would resort to one of Thomas Wilson's dance manuals. The dance master at the King's Theatre Opera House in London, Wilson, considered dancing to be 'the most enchanting of all human amusements, it is the parent of joy and the soul and support of cheerfulness; it banishes grief, and cheers the evening hours of those who have studied or laboured in the day and brings with it a mixture of delightful sensations which enrapture the senses'. With a far less eloquent title, his first manual *An Analysis of Country Dancing*

'Almacks' from *Life in London* by Pierce Egan (1822). Nothing less than formal full dress was acceptable at the prestigious Almack's Club as the Duke of Wellington discovered to his chagrin when even he was turned away for wearing trousers rather than formal full dress with breeches in 1814.

'Dancing Dress', *Ackermann's Repository of Arts* (February 1809). The head is ornamented with bandeaus of frosted gold; gold necklace earrings and armlets; white satin opera dress trimmed all round with gold, tied in front with a gold cord and tassel; white satin shoes trimmed in gold, white elbow length gloves and fan edged in gold.

Wherein are Displayed all the Figures Ever Used in Country Dances, in a Way so Easy and Familiar, That Persons of the Meanest Capacity May in a Short Time Acquire (Without the Aid of a Master) a Complete Knowledge of That Rational and Polite Amusement was published in 1808, complete with diagrams of how to master the steps and how the dance formations should look. Fourteen more followed, and his works remained the key terpsichorean texts until the 1850s.

From the French *contredanse*, referring to the way the dancers faced each other, usually across a long narrow ballroom, the country dance was a feature at every ball. The steps were quite simple and, as it took a long time for each couple to take their turn, it could be an opportunity to 'stand up with' a chosen partner for up to half an hour of flirtatious conversation, albeit in safe sight of the whole community. A great pleasure with the right person, but dancing could be an ordeal if asked by someone as tedious as Mr Collins in *Pride and Prejudice*, who requests the first two dances with Elizabeth at the Netherfield ball. Etiquette demands that she must agree or forfeit her chances of dancing with others later.

Jane Austen had fond memories of dancing the cotillion, which had its heyday in her youth. It fell from fashion later but remained popular enough for especially dedicated cotillion balls to continue at the Assembly Rooms in Bath. Catherine Morland enjoys attending one and no doubt 'the rapid changes of the cotillion admirably calculated for the display of elegant gaiety,' as it was described in *The Mirror of the Graces* in 1811.

The balls of Jane's youth would begin with a minuet, a favourite of Louis XIV, still regarded as the apex of elegant dancing. Sadly, as with most aspects of the *ancien régime*, it was dealt a fatal blow at the French Revolution, although it remained the foundation of dance education.

76

The quadrille was introduced at Almack's by Lady Jersey in 1815 and it quickly became a firm favourite as it was similar to the energetic cotillion but with easier steps. As the country assemblies Jane attended were rather behind London fashions, it is likely that she did not dance the quadrille, but her niece Fanny Knight sent her sheet music. Jane wrote to her in February 1817: 'Much obliged for the quadrilles, which I am grown to think pretty enough, though of course they are inferior to the Cotillions of my own day.' Jane had made the transition, as many more mature ladies did, from dancer to accompanist.

Waltz-mania spread like wildfire from Vienna to Paris during the 1790s, gaining a notorious reputation as countless young people danced themselves into a frenzy of excitement. The older generation disapproved, citing that they were inviting illness going from the passionate exertion of the overheated ballroom into the snowy night without proper warm clothes or shoes. Worse still was the shocking moral laxity it promoted as the waltz was often danced in a drunken frenzy, with the dancers expressing every variety of human passion. Goethe wrote that 'none but husbands and wives can with any propriety be partners in the waltz'.

The waltz came to London with Wellington's officers, who had enjoyed the breathless delights while stationed in Europe. The controversy came in attendance, only heightening the excited anticipation with which the waltz was greeted. *Mirror Of The Graces* agreed with Goethe, warning: 'There is something in the close approximation of persons, in the attitudes, and in the motion, which ill agrees with the delicacy of woman, should she be placed in a situation with any other man than the most intimate connection she can have in life.'

As with all matters of ballroom etiquette, the waltz was not accepted until it was danced at Almack's, and that was not until 1815. Lord Byron wrote of 'hands which may freely range in public sight', which he probably meant as more of a recommendation for the waltz, but in his 1816 *A Description of the Correct Method of Waltzing* Thomas Wilson reassured that it was 'not an enemy of true morals' and would not 'endanger virtue'. It did, however, change the context of dancing. All the other dances included a social element where partners were exchanged briefly or there was a moment to talk as well as to dance.

'Parisian Dancers No. 2 L' Horatia', published for *La Belle Assemblée* (No. 137, 1 July 1820). The description explains: 'The music of this dance is the favourite Quadrille air of L'Horatia,' and goes on to describe the figures required to perform it. It was essential to dance correctly to avoid compromising other dancers, and frequently a practice ball was held a few days before a prestigious public ball to ensure everyone knew their steps.

'La Folie du Jour' by Louis Leopold Boilly (Paris, 18 February 1797). Enjoying a romantic moment lost in their dance, their folly is that they fail to spot that their drunken accompanist cannot tear his lascivious gaze away from the girl's legs glimpsed to the thigh through her ultra-sheer muslin skirts and her naked toes in neoclassical sandals.

The overall result was to fill the ballroom with an elegant design of dancers pleasing to participants and onlookers alike – a communal experience. The waltz created romance, an insular experience of a couple within a crowd yet alone with eyes only for each other.

It was one thing to share a blissful spark of romance, but it was quite another to nurture it into a loving proposal, especially while fully chaperoned. How to make such a life altering choice with such a limited exchange of information?

In *Northanger Abbey* Henry Tilney is warm and charming as well as good looking, and Catherine openly falls for him. He is also kind and considerate as well as good humoured, as evidenced by his concern for Mrs Allen's damaged muslin, and Catherine is justified in her choice.

In *Sense and Sensibility* Elinor teases Marianne because she so obviously delights in finding that she and Willoughby share a passion for the poetry of Cowper and the novels of Sir Walter Scott and rushes to confirm all that they share and adore. These shared sensibilities might be an excellent foundation for their relationship, but Elinor fears that romantic passion might lead them to deceive themselves. This is certainly true of Willoughby, who charms Marianne and her mother so successfully that they both expect a proposal is imminent. Elinor takes no pleasure in being proved right to be circumspect, and almost loses her own beau, Edward, because by contrast she is far too reticent in expressing her emotions.

Although a chaperone could hinder a proposal, in the brightly romantic world of *Emma*, our heroine is an active facilitator to love in her role of chaperone – albeit according to her own misguided rules. In such tight-knit, gossip-fuelled circles it was necessary to make sure that a young lady wasn't compromised and her reputation damaged. It is yet another

'An evening at Frascati' (1809). All seem to be enjoying socialising, except for the woman to the left, the chaperone – usually slightly older than her charge and without any romantic opportunities of her own to distract her.

example of John Thorpe's selfish boorishness that he compromises Catherine by whisking her off in his carriage against her protestations and without a chaperone.

Swept off her feet, the headstrong Lydia Bennet elopes with the roguish George Wickham with no thought other than the excitement of it all. She would be 'ruined' if it were not for Mr Darcy's intervention, and the scandal that she thoughtlessly, wilfully courts would be a shameful taint that would follow all her sisters, as the odious Mr Collins writes to Mr Bennet: 'I am inclined to think that her own disposition must be naturally bad ... this false step in one daughter will be injurious to the fortunes of all the others; for who, as lady Catherine herself condescendingly says, will connect themselves with such a family?'

In *Pride and Prejudice* Charlotte Lucas expresses that happiness in marriage is a matter of pure chance and 'if the dispositions of the parties are ever so well known to each other ... they always continue to grow sufficiently unlike afterwards to have their share of vexation; and it is better to know as little as possible of the defects of the person with whom you are to pass your life'.

In a tiny way Jane also threw propriety to the wind when she was entranced by Tom Lefroy in January 1796. She wrote excitedly to Cassandra: 'Imagine to yourself everything most profligate and shocking in the way of dancing and sitting down together.' She was aware that she was 'being particular', allowing him too much individual attention as she danced with him almost exclusively at three consecutive balls, delighting in their shared love of literature and falling for his deep blue eyes. She even ventured to write to Cassandra: 'I look forward with great impatience to it, as I rather expect to receive an offer from my friend in the course of the evening.' But sadly no offer came. She and Marianne had both left themselves unprotected when they fell in love, and both suffered heart-breaking disappointment when they were abandoned for women with wealth.

On 2 December 1802 Jane finally received her proposal; unfortunately, it was not from Tom. Harris Bigg Wither was the shy little brother of Jane's friends, Alethea and Catherine Bigg. Plain, slightly awkward and uncouth with a stammer, he was no romantic hero. He was, however, of a good family that Jane had known since childhood and he was heir to the medieval Manydown Park estate. Given the terribly precarious position she and her mother would be in when her father died, it is no wonder that she agreed to his proposal

'Jealousy – The Rival' by Thomas Rowlandson, *c.* 1790. With so few eligible gentlemen to choose from, jealousy could be fraught. One young lady wrote in 1800 of the extreme and unfair competition on the marriage market with 'the married women in this licentious age who engross the men to themselves and hinder us poor girls from getting husbands'.

out of the blue. She undoubtedly suffered a sleepless night worrying over what marriage to a man she did not love would bring, and in the morning she retracted her promise. It was a sad, humiliating episode and an opportunity to gain security missed, but Jane's family were supportive and the friendship with the Biggs survived.

If there were no proposals forthcoming before a young lady reached her quarter century her prospects started to look increasingly bleak. She could, like Charlotte Lucas, accept a proposal from an odious fool like Mr Collins and spend the rest of her life hiding in the lesser parlour to avoid hearing his misanthropic opinions. She might gain a modicum of independence as the lady of her own home, but she would undoubtedly be dragged into his uncontrollable sycophancy to Lady Catherine.

If she had a small income she might be able to set up her own small home like Miss Bates in *Emma*, who only has her deaf mother to contend with. The most striking example of successful domestic independence is that of the ladies of Llangollen – Lady Eleanor Butler and Sarah Ponsonby. Eleanor's parents despaired of their bluestocking daughter ever taking a husband, and Sarah was fearful of her licentious, old, supposed guardian attempting to take advantage of her, so they took fate into their own hands and dressed as men armed with pistols and ran away together. They retired into romantic solitude to Plas Newydd, a cottage near Llangollen, where they created a beautiful home together – complete with shell grotto – and lived independently of social convention. In so doing they became celebrities of the age, visited by everyone from the Duke of Wellington to Wordsworth. They were even awarded a pension by George III.

Mostly, spinsterhood was thought rather tragic and these spare, single women were burdens to be distributed within the more successful households of the family. Frequently, in exchange for food and board, sequestered in often what was little better than a housekeeper's room, they were obliged to make themselves useful as something little more than a glorified servant. They would see a brother inherit everything yet grant her only pin money; they would look after the children they would never have; and they would be invited to parties but only after they had organised them, and even then only to play for the dancers.

In *Sense and Sensibility*, Marianne's heartbreak is so acute she falls desperately ill, and sadly she was not the only one to fade into a dramatic decline from a broken heart. Proportionately, there were more young men lost during the Napoleonic Wars than even the First World War, so with such a shortage of potential husbands many young women lost all chance of love and marriage and went into a grieving decline, a sort of staged version of consumption that involved a lot of languorous sighing while reclining on an elegantly proportioned day bed comforted only by Gothic novels and romantic poetry. Going into decline was a way of reclaiming one's life and creating a role within the family where there wasn't one. There was at least some romance in being poor Aunt Olivia who went into decline and remained there as Dicken's Miss Havisham would later do, rather than poor Aunt Olivia who has to earn her keep as unpaid housekeeper or governess in her brother's home.

'Evening Mourning Dress', *Ackermann's Repository of Arts* (December 1810). Princess Amelia had recently died of tuberculosis, on 2 November, prompting a spate of mourning fashions to be worn during state mourning including mourning dress for formal evening occasions because, sadly, even a broken heart couldn't jeopardise the hunt for a husband.

'Heart Stealing – I've Got It' by W. Derby, *c.* 1820. A young lady whose heart has been stolen by cupid dreams only of love and romance, but with love unfulfilled decline is sure to follow.

7

Illicit Pleasures

FULL DRESS

'Full Dress, Parisian Ladies in their Winter Dress for 1800' by John Cawse (published 24 November 1799 by S. W. Fores, No. 50 Piccadilly). Satirical drawing making fun of the reticule, or 'ridicule', and the vogue for scanty and revealing diaphanous muslins – so revealing there is a bare bottom and bare bosom.

As the figurehead of the era, the Prince Regent made little attempt to conceal that his pleasures extended to those definitely not approved of by the moral majority. His Carlton House set was populated by some of the most brilliant minds of the day, but also some of the most louche and licentious. Among the politicians and scholars there were drunkards, gamblers and courtesans.

Princess Caroline, as the Prince Regent's new bride, noted that her husband's 'blackguard companions … were constantly drunk and filthy, sleeping and snoring in boots on the sofas'. Although initially appalled, seemingly the princess took a 'can't beat them join them attitude' and in 1814 she took a lover, an Italian adventurer called Pergami. She took up residence with the former general's valet in Genoa where they drove each day in a phaeton shaped like a seashell. Jane Austen wrote: 'Poor woman, I shall support her as long as I can because she is a woman, and because I hate her husband … she would have been respectable, if the prince had behaved only tolerably to her at first.'

Those that were happy to turn a blind eye to the Prince Regent's unsavoury activities were unabashed in bashing his wife, and the scandal only worsened in 1820 when she returned expecting to join her husband for his coronation only to find that she was locked out of the ceremony. The prince instead had his current lover, Lady Conyngham ('Cunning Ham', as she was dubbed by contemporary satirists), in a place of honour at his coronation banquet where he could nod and wink at her throughout the proceedings.

Sexual profligacy was almost encouraged as part of a 'boys will be boys' machismo, and as the prince's affairs were widely known it gave licence for many men to follow suit. Even his first youthful dalliances with Perdita Robinson were conducted in full view of everyone – including her husband – at Vauxhall Gardens.

Many men took their pleasure at the expense of the women they purported to love, but there were those who got their own back. Hariette Wilson became a notorious courtesan with the publication of her *Memoires* in 1825; they would run to several volumes as she revealed details of her relationships with some of the most eminent men of the Regency.

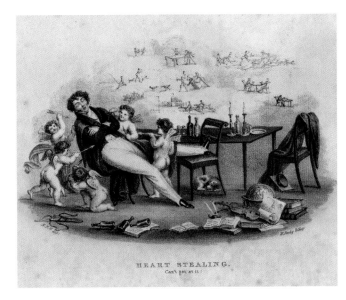

'Heart Stealing – Can't Get At It' by W. Derby (c. 1820). The young gentleman has filled his life with gambling, sports, joyous drinking and japes, with perhaps a little learning, thereby making himself immune to love.

She had fallen on hard times when the promises of financial support from various of her former beaux had not been forthcoming. To remind them, she and her publisher, John Joseph Stockdale, provided them with the opportunity to make a settlement so as to not have their particular liaison included. Many did, but the Duke of Wellington famously replied, 'Publish and be damned!' He was sent to London to answer for the many crimes he had committed there, under a series of assumed identities.

Throughout the eighteenth century it had become the height of romance to make an impassioned love match and elope rather than submit to the rigours of family marriage brokering. Couples would make a moonlight flit to the chapel at the Fleet Prison or all the way to Gretna Green to make their match, frequently not realising that such marriages were not necessarily legal.

One such elopement ended with dire consequences in 1791 at Vauxhall Gardens in Duddeston, near Birmingham. A handsome young gentleman claiming to be Captain Mouson of the dragoons arrived at the hotel attached to the gardens and booked in with a very pretty, very young girl, claiming that she was his bride and they had just eloped. The next day her irate father arrived with six officers of the local militia, burst into the couple's room and attempted to rescue her. For the newlyweds this horrific intrusion and attempted kidnapping was intolerable, and he threatened her father. Shots were fired, resulting in one of the officers shot in the face, the musket ball smashing six of his teeth, and Mouson was arrested. When he was next seen – in a Birmingham prison cell – a few days later it was clear that he had sustained a terrible beating. All the papers reported extensively about the trial and many people came to court in Warwick to catch a glimpse of the handsome young rogue who had stolen this young girl's heart and, it would appear, had also defrauded half of London's finest tailors under the stolen identity of the Duke of Ormond. The ladies that attended the court in ever-increasing numbers petitioned for his release as they asserted no fair trial could take place with him still suffering so severely from his injuries after having been thrown down the stairs by his guards, but to no avail. He was sent to London to answer for his many crimes there, committed under a number of assumed identities.

'A Morning Visit to A Young Templar'. If it were not clear enough from the knowing looks and arch dialogue that the young student has been caught *en flagrante*, the pattens – generally only worn by servants and tradeswomen by the early nineteenth century – abandoned in the hall and the reflection of the young woman in the bedroom confirm the secret assignation.

During the trial his real identity was discovered, and it was James Molesworth Hubbard of Virginia who was sentenced to death at the Old Bailey. He promptly ordered a new suit for his execution at Newgate in February 1793, promising the tailor whose rooms were opposite the prison, that it would be worth his while as his execution would gather such a crowd of young ladies that he could charge them half a crown each to take a prime viewing spot at his windows that overlooked the prison yard.

There were, of course, some blackguards who knew exactly that once married a lady's fortune became her husband's. This was a fact that George Wickham was well aware of when he attempted to elope with Darcy's fifteen-year-old sister. Had he succeeded the embarrassment engendered by denying the match would have been too acute to do anything other than accept him into the family.

It was another motive entirely that prompted him to elope with Lydia Bennet. She is so frivolous and in love with love, as well as with the handsome Wickham, that she fails to consider that for it to be an elopement rather than a disgrace their first stop after leaving Brighton had to be to get married. Unbeknown to Lydia, instead of neglecting their nuptials through frivolous negligence, Wickham is deliberately avoiding marriage as he still intends to marry an heiress as soon as he can secure one.

It was only Darcy's caring intervention that prevented Lydia's reputation – and consequently that of all her family – from being ruined. The fate for those who had no such guardian was wretched. No longer accepted into polite society, women were forced to seek a protector to keep them. In some cases – as with Emma Hamilton – it was a successful arrangement, and social ignominy was exchanged for an attractive lifestyle and a freedom not enjoyed by most women. But in many others a succession of protectors became a succession of clients as mistress became courtesan, then finally prostitute.

'Last Parisian Full Dress', *La Belle Assemblée* (No. 3, 1 April 1810). Evening dress usually includes nothing more than a light shawl to add warmth to a diaphanous gown, but this 'Zealand wrap of pink satin bordered with a rich wide trimming of swansdown with a Kamskatska mantlet of correspondent fur' looks warm and perfect for doing a moonlight flit to Gretna Green.

'Lady Emma Hamilton as Ambassadress', after George Romney, *c.* 1791. Her work as ambassadress to the court of Naples was pivotal in the success of the war effort. Lord Nelson freely acknowledged that he could not have succeeded without her and requested that George III ensure she was cared for after his death. Tragically, the king refused due to her 'fallen' status and she died in poverty, forgotten and alone.

It was estimated that there were 50,000 prostitutes in London and many of them circulated through the unsavoury haunts of gin shops and seedy 'gambling hells'. They entertained soldiers or sailors on leave hoping for a few laughs, a dance and maybe a meal before retiring to such places as 'Gropecunt Lane'. These despicable back alleys were also the final refuge of prostitutes too ravaged to put their looks on display, who would make their transactions with those already blind drunk or who might pickpocket those too intent upon their lust to notice the loss.

Pierce Egan has his heroes meet some beautiful Cyprians at the theatre. Named for the pleasure-seeking devotees of Aphrodite on Cyprus, they were prostitutes of a higher order. Dressed beautifully, they promoted their charms at the theatre, taking a prominent box so they were seen well-lit by those who chose to ogle them instead of watching the play, or being delightful company for the gentlemen who clamoured to meet them in the private saloon at the Covent Garden Theatre. They were in the orbit of gentlemen and many eventually made fortuitous marriages or sufficient savings that they were able to start a small business of their own. They were nevertheless utterly under the control of the Bawd, for whom they worked. To the extent that even the attractive clothes they wore were loaned for the night at a fee to be taken from their earnings. To ensure there was no possibility of selling, pawning or damaging the finery, let alone the chance of escape, they were also constantly followed.

The White House in Soho Square was one of the more fashionable brothels. Once an elegant aristocratic home, its well-proportioned rooms were opulently decorated and themed by colour – one entirely gold, another entirely silver and a third bronze. Other more private rooms were themed as the painted chamber, the grotto, the coal hole and the

'The Saloon at the Covent Garden Theatre', from *Life in London* by Pierce Egan (1822). The 'Cyprians' presented their cards to eligible gentlemen stating that they were seeking new 'rich friends' or clients.

skeleton room – with a real skeleton in the closet. Each was equipped with mirrors from all angles and a wide array of peculiar devices to satisfy every desire.

Although most of the eighteenth-century secret societies such as the Hellfire Club had faded into history, the Beggar's Club was still leading the way in debauchery. Masturbation was condemned by the medical establishment and increasingly by wider society as it was thought to cause infertility, seizures, impotence and possibly gonorrhoea. The Beggar's Benison were well prepared to take the risk, and the secret society founded in Scotland in the 1780s based their tenets around the shared pleasure of onanism, providing a well-stocked library of pornography, lectures about anatomy and sex, and even 'pose girls' at their meetings who would create erotic tableau for their viewing pleasure.

Homosexuality had been illegal since the sixteenth century, but there was a new rash of convictions as the eighteenth century drew to a close. It might have been part of a more general move towards moral order, but attitudes in general were becoming increasingly anti-homosexual. William Beckford created an unholy scandal with the homoerotic subtext of his novel *Vathek the Vampire*, published in 1796. Beckford had an education rich in both Eastern and European classics and, fresh from a Grand Tour that included Turkey and Constantinople, his vampire caliph was tinged with the 'exotic'. This was a familiar motif in eighteenth-century literature and, although suggestive of the erotic, it was not too scandalous in itself. The problem was that two years earlier Beckford had been caught in a compromising position with a beautiful young man – some said in flagrante – and many in polite society shunned him.

After the tragic death of his young wife, Beckford retreated behind the imposing high walls of Fonthill Abbey to carve his own life as he redesigned and rebuilt his palatial home. Despite his incredible creation with its legendary tower, the taint of scandal remained as he chose to live, like Vathek, with only a young male partner.

Where Beckford retreated from the speculation, Lord Byron positively courted any rumour that would add to his reputation as 'mad, bad, and dangerous to know'. While women's pleasure in the thrills of Gothic literature were widely mocked and frowned upon, Lord Bryon took his Gothic pleasures to extremes. During the most decadent

[1905]

This beautiful white tulle ensemble from *Le Journal et des Dames at des Modes Costumes Parisiens* (1821), complete with Elizabethan ruff, was undoubtedly inspired by the thrills of Gothic literature.

years of the eighteenth century his great uncle, the fifth lord known as 'the Wicked Lord Byron', had drawn upon the traditions of the Hellfire Club to stage orgies at Newstead Abbey, their family seat in Nottinghamshire. Not to be outdone, once he inherited the poet was rumoured to have recommenced the tradition, upping the ante of outrage in the increasingly pious age by including 'Satanic rites'.

Newstead Abbey had been decommissioned during Henry VIII's Reformation in the most hideous, brutal fashion, with most of the monks murdered and their hallowed relics stolen or thrown into the lake. Their bodies had been hastily buried in the abbey grounds and, as a crowning touch for his depravities, the poet had recovered one of their skulls and had it fashioned into a goblet.

Byron's poor monk was not the only one to have his head misused. As recently confirmed, despite Shakespeare taking the trouble to apply a curse to anyone who might tamper with his grave, his skull disappeared at some point during the eighteenth century. A Victorian account discreetly only related after the protagonists had died tells of a plot set in the autumn of 1794. There were more than a few rakish gentlemen with human skulls gracing their cabinets of curiosities. Many were ancient relics gathered on the Grand Tour, but a growing number were far more modern and procured through dangerous liaisons with 'resurrection men' – those who, like the notorious Burke and Hare, would disinter human remains to sell. Reputedly, Sir Horace Walpole had allowed it to slip that he would be happy to pay 300 guineas to whoever could procure the Bard's legendary dome, while David Garrick had made a similar offer after his Shakespeare Jubilee. According to the second part of the story, neither gentleman was willing to fulfil their offer. The skull snatchers' attempts to restore it to Shakespeare's grave in Holy Trinity Church were disturbed, leaving them no choice but to reinter it elsewhere – the

Lord Byron in Albanian dress, engraved by William Finden after Thomas Philips (c. 1820). Byron visited Albania in 1809 as part of his Grand Tour. He stayed with the ruler Ali Pasha, writing in a letter to his mother that Albanian costume was 'the most magnificent in the world' and sending home several traditional suits to lend an exotic air to his wild reputation.

account suggests a small village church in Warwickshire, near Alcester – and the skull still remains missing.

Heavy drinking was very popular for men throughout the Regency and many gentlemen were proud to claim that they were 'three bottle men', avowing that they could easily see off three bottles of port or claret within a single evening. This seemingly impossible amount was achievable as bottles were around two thirds of our modern 75 cl and the wines were not fermented as long to attain such a strength, but port was fortified with brandy.

Unsurprisingly, heavy drinking was also very popular with young men taking a break from their university studies to visit London. Heavy drinking led to roister-toistering revel-routs, which often resulted in appalling behaviour. Pierce Egan in *Life in London* describes the popular drunken pastime of 'boxing the watch'. There was a nightwatchman, or 'Charley', in most London parishes to ensure law and order and to call out the hours throughout the night. Often the Charley was more interested in napping, huddled inside his sentry box than in keeping the peace, so it was great sport for the drunken reveller to creep up behind and tip the box to land door-side down with the poor Charley still in it. The revellers would then run riot smashing windows, stealing hackney cab horses or yelling 'fire!' knowing full well that it would take ages for a Charley from another parish to arrive. Sometimes they were caught and hauled before the magistrates the next day; otherwise, they headed to a coffee house in Covent Garden cheekily dubbed 'the Finish' where they could share tales over coffee before promptly falling asleep.

Drunkenness was perfectly acceptable within the upper classes as a masculine rite of passage, but for those further down the social scale – with arguably far more reason to resort to drink – it was widely condemned. Like Pierce Egan's heroes Tom and Jerry, there were many young men out on a revel-rout who enjoyed visiting sleazy gin shops to sample the 'blue ruin'. Along with many ugly names like a 'kick in the guts' or 'rag water' because it reduced the drinker quickly to rags, gin was often referred to as 'blue ruin'. This referenced the ghastly, ghostly hue of the cadaverous hollow eyes and blue-tinged lips induced by methanol poisoning, leading to blindness and death. As cheap gin was frequently distilled

'Scene at the Breaking up of a Fashionable Rout' (published by T Kelly, No. 17 Paternoster Row, 26 July 1822). Revel-routs were irresistible fun to some, the scourge of a night out to others and a nuisance to the nightwatch, who had to try to break up fights between fashionable gentlemen without offending them.

'Boxing The Watch' from *Life in London* by Pierce Egan (1822). A favourite 'sport' for drunken revellers on their way home.

from old potatoes rather than grain, the skins could attract bacteria to produce dangerously poisonous levels of methanol. It was also common for the gin to be made too acidic, allowing it to be contaminated with copper salts, giving a blue tinge.

In 1799 it was Humphrey Davy, future inventor of the Davy lamp and president of the Royal Society, who first investigated the effects of breathing nitrous oxide and reported sensations of 'thrilling and pleasure' of varying intensities. He performed many other investigations and found himself seduced into frequent recreational use of the gas. He shared his findings with his close friend, the poet Samuel Taylor Coleridge, who recorded: 'The first time I inspired the nitrous oxide, I felt a highly pleasurable sensation of warmth over my whole frame ... The only motion which I felt inclined to make, was that of laughing at those who were looking at me. My eyes felt distended, and towards the last, my heart beat as if it were leaping up and down. On removing the mouth-piece, the whole sensation went off almost instantly.' Quite a profound impression upon a man not unfamiliar with opium.

Robert Southey, future Poet Laureate, wrote to his brother: 'Humphrey Davy has actually invented a new pleasure for which language has no name ... I am going for more this evening – it makes one so strong and so happy! Oh excellent air bag ... I am sure the air in heaven must be this wonder working gas of delight'. With such rave reactions it was no surprise that everyone wanted to try it, and under the colloquialism 'laughing gas' there were lectures and shows at theatres and fairgrounds exhibiting its effects, as well as parties to fully enjoy the euphoria and mild hallucinations.

'Blue Ruin at the Gin Shop' from *Life in London* by Pierce Egan (1822). Most of the drinkers seem happily oblivious, ignoring the woman who feeds gin to her baby and the cadaverous old drunk who clings to the vat of 'Old Tom'.

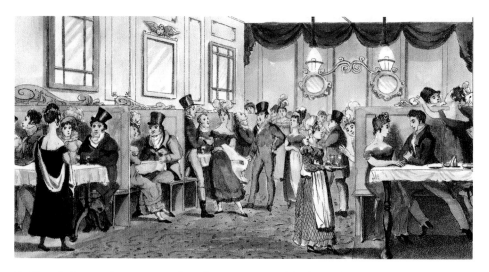

'A Noted Oyster Room near the Theatres at 3 o'clock in the Morning' (published by T. Kelly, No. 17 Paternoster Row, 23 February 1823). The finish of the evening would mean cheap and casual food and possibly the opportunity to make the chance acquaintance of a lady of the town.

'New Discoveries in Pneumatics!' Leading members of the Royal Institution satirised by James Gilray (1802). The effects of nitrous oxide were noted in *Ackermann's Repository of Arts* in February 1811: 'We have heard it asserted by those who have inhaled it that: "It was the best boon the gods had lent to man" and reported that: "Under the operation of inhaling the nitrous oxide we appear to feel a more than momentary bliss; to be exhilarated not by 'ideal gales' but 'redolent of joy and youth to breathe life's second spring"'.

Conclusion

'Carlton House' by A. C. Pugin and J. Bluck from Ackermann's *Microcosm of London* (1808). When Jane visited on 13 November 1815, the prince's librarian, Revd James Stanier Clarke, gave her a tour of the library, which included her books, and perhaps the armoury, which included an encyclopaedic collection of international military uniforms and boots as well as weaponry.

Above left: 'St James's Palace' by A. C. Pugin and J. Bluck from Ackermann's *Microcosm of London* (1808). The king or queen's 'Drawing Room' was the most prestigious event of all, where young ladies were formally presented at court, thereby making them eligible for aristocratic marriage proposals.

Above right: 'Court Dress with the New Hoop', invented by Mrs Bell for *La Belle Assemblée* (No. 97, 1 June 1817). Unfortunately the court hoop became rather farcical after the introduction of the elevated waistline but Mrs Bell's invention would change all that: it 'enables a lady to sit comfortably in a sedan, or other carriage, while the hoop is worn, with the same ease as any other garment; and by this unique and unrivalled novelty the splendor and dignity of Court costume is not only preserved, but considerably heightened.'

The conundrum of the Prince Regent, at once an erudite patron of the arts but also a porcine reprobate, is the conundrum of the era that bears his name. He loved Jane's works so much that he invited her dedicate *Emma* to him at a meeting at Carlton House in November 1815, and he kept a set of her novels at each of his homes.

Although his involvement with fashion, through Beau Brummell, and his contribution to military grandeur were thoroughly mocked, his gift of the Angerstein Collection formed the core of the National Gallery, which opened in 1824. He was proud to make a contribution to the culture of his era, stating that his collection of art was not for his pleasure alone, 'but to gratify the public taste, and lay before the artist the best specimens for his study.' He also donated his father's entire 85,000-volume library to the British Museum and founded the Royal Society of Literature.

With the plans the Regent commissioned from John Nash, London was transformed into a beautifully laid out royal capital rather than the home to countless shopkeepers that Napoleon had criticised. Thousands of miles of canal and turnpike road were laid, linking the capital with all major cities and the burgeoning industrial North, at first to supply the war effort, but eventually ushering in a new era of prosperity founded on technology, travel and communication.

Right: 'The Hall and Staircase, British Museum' by A. C. Pugin and J. Bluck from Ackermann's *Microcosm of London* (1808). Once the home of the Duke of Montague, as Walpole described, 'the spacious and lofty magnificence of the apartments' was well suited to house the incredible collections of literature, art, antiquity and natural history, including a 21-foot-long crocodile on the stairs.

Below: 'Regent Street', *Ackermann's Repository of Arts* (1822). The view looking toward the colonnade was one of several views of the exciting development of Regent Street, the most fashionable street in London. Contemporary critics complained that Nash was profligate with his use of columns, complaining: 'Columns are only used in the same way that some plain women wear more showy ornaments than their beauty because they are substitutes for it, and hide defects.'

Promenade Costume, *Ackermann's Repository of Arts* (September 1813). Although also perfect for reading, it was described as: 'A Promenade Costume of white jaconet muslin high dress, with long sleeves and collar of needle-work; a Pyrennean mantle, of pomona green sarsnet, trimmed with Spanish fringe confined in graceful folds on the left shoulder'. Accessorised with 'a white lace veil thrown over the head-dress. A large Eastern parasol with deep Chinese awning. Roman shoes, or Spanish slipper, of pomona green kid, or jean. Gloves of primrose or amber-coloured kid.'